Anthony Wigens is the founder of Country College in Hertfordshire and lives on the edge of Welwyn Garden City. Near his house is a farm, and it put in his mind his inalienable right, based on the Common Law, to run a clandestine farm from the hedgerows and waste areas round about.

*Anthony Wigens*

# The Clandestine Farm

A PALADIN BOOK

**GRANADA**
London Toronto Sydney New York

Published by Granada Publishing Limited in 1981

ISBN 0 586 08305 7

A Granada Paperback Original


Granada Publishing Limited
Frogmore, St Albans, Herts AL2 2NF
and
3 Upper James Street, London W1R 4BP
866 United Nations Plaza, New York, NY 10017, USA
117 York Street, Sydney, NSW 2000, Australia
100 Skyway Avenue, Rexdale, Ontario, M9W 3A6, Canada
PO Box 84165, Greenside, 2034 Johannesburg, South Africa
61 Beach Road, Auckland, New Zealand

Set, printed and bound in Great Britain by
Cox & Wyman Ltd, Reading
Set in Intertype Plantin

## *Contents*


1 Over the fence 11

2 Lockleys Farm 19

3 Forgive us our trespasses 30

4 Private land and common rights 41

5 Good King Henry 48

6 Hunter's moon 60

7 Autumn 75

8 The bracken battle 92

9 The woods 100

10 The Roman snail 112

11 Winter 121

12 Roots 128

Bibliography 139

To George Baron, yeoman farmer extraordinary, who held title to the Clandestine Farm

We shall not cease from exploration
And the end of all our exploring
Will be to arrive where we started
And know the place for the first time.

T. S. Eliot

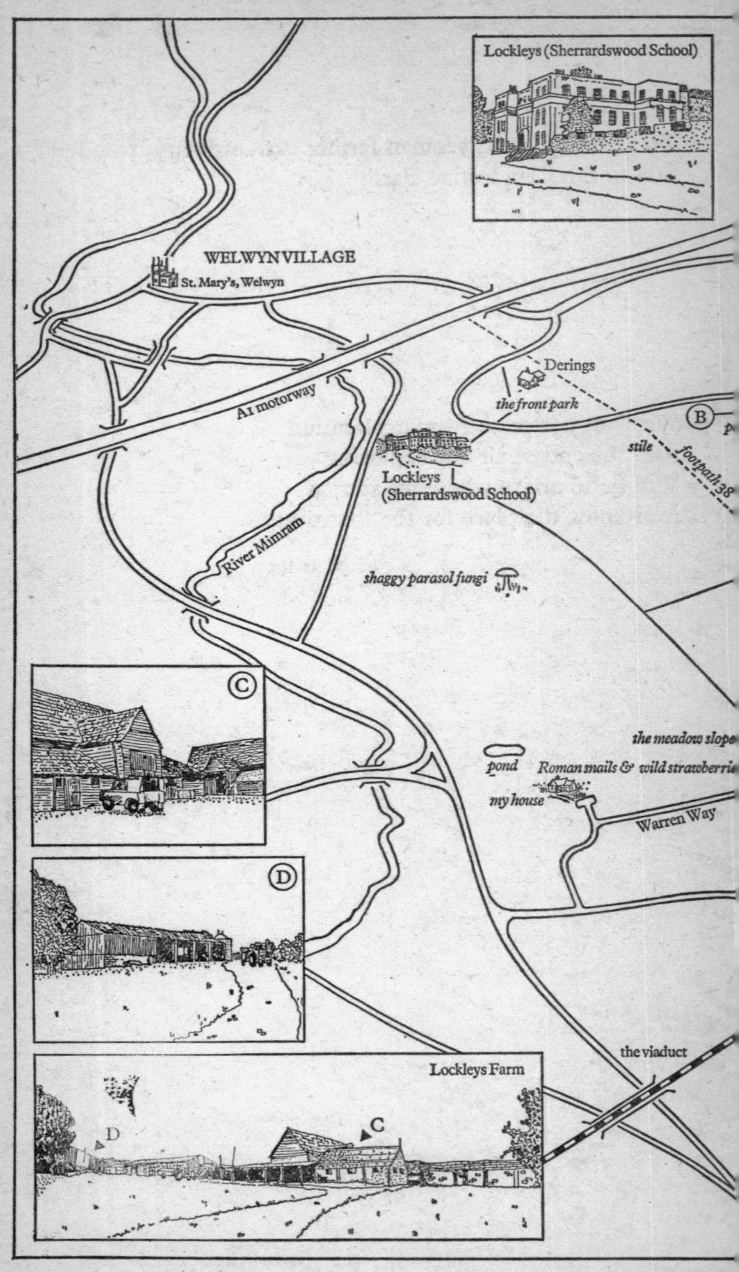
Lockleys (Sherrardswood School)
WELWYN VILLAGE
St. Mary's, Welwyn
A1 motorway
Derings
the front park
B
stile
footpath 38
Lockleys
(Sherrardswood School)
River Mimram
shaggy parasol fungi
C
the meadow slope
pond
Roman snails & wild strawberri
my house
Warren Way
D
the viaduct
Lockleys Farm
D
C

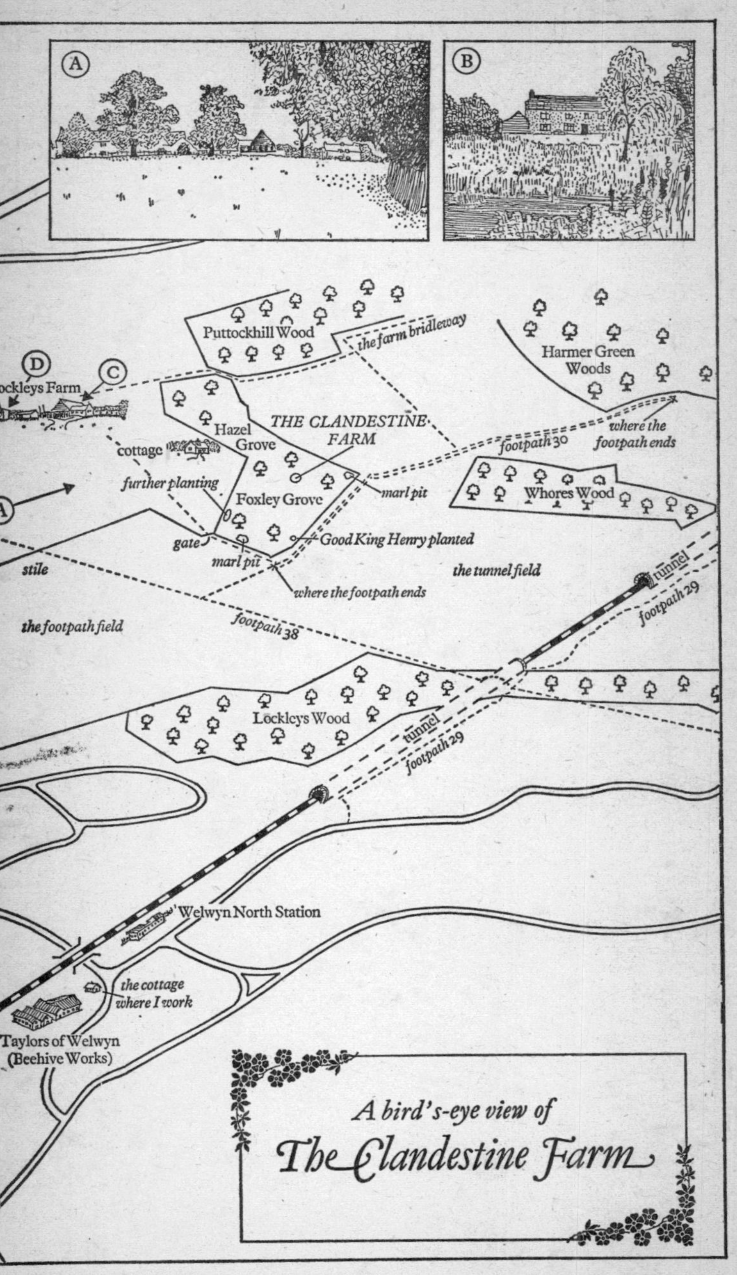
A
B
Puttockhill Wood
the farm bridleway
Harmer Green Woods
D
C
ockleys Farm
Hazel Grove
THE CLANDESTINE FARM
cottage
footpath 30
where the footpath ends
further planting
Foxley Grove
marl pit
Whores Wood
A
gate
Good King Henry planted
marl pit
stile
the tunnel field
where the footpath ends
tunnel
footpath 29
the footpath field
footpath 38
Lockleys Wood
tunnel
footpath 29
Welwyn North Station
the cottage where I work
Taylors of Welwyn (Beehive Works)
A bird's-eye view of
The Clandestine Farm

# 1 Over the fence

One March afternoon I climbed over the fence which divides my neighbour's land from mine, and walked on his farm as though it were my own. I looked on it, not in a jealous, possessive way, but simply as I might if there were no such thing as land property and all the people held all the land in common. This was to be the Clandestine Farm, a stretch of countryside from which I would take a portion of the natural produce without asking any man's leave. To do so I trespassed on the legal owner's land, but I took none of the crops which he grew and did nothing to harm them or restrict his privileges. I neither squatted nor expropriated, nor was I a thief.

Just for a moment, I invite you to forget what you learned at school in history lessons, the saga of men's efforts to control the earth as their property. Consider this: The land was here before us and will outlive us. The land is not inanimate, it owns us, and we are just some of its creatures. The land lends us minerals, feeds us, clothes us, houses us – if we have the will to work – and when we die it takes back all it has given. If you can accept that statement even momentarily before the 'yes, buts' come flooding into your mind, conditioned by all that history, for that moment you may understand why I encourage those who 'own' no land, to trespass.

People who are too arrogant to accept that the land is their master parcel it up and say 'this is my farm', 'this is my forest' and they trade with us and amongst themselves with the products the land has lent them. Their myths are the foundation of the society into which you and I were born, and the few preempt the resource which all need for life itself: land.

If you love the land and are content simply to walk, to breathe country air and enjoy country sights, then your battle is for right of access, for public footpaths and waymarked routes through the most beautiful parts of the countryside. But for me, it is not enough simply to visit the land. I want to accept all its gifts, spiritual and material, and I want them direct – not processed and packed by someone else and always with a price tag.

The farmer makes a deal with us, providing the food which sets us free to travel from the lands which could support us; but it is no contract, and the deal need last no longer than we want it to. To be separated from the earth now would be intolerable for me. I must have access to it, and usually treat any ordinary fence or warning notice as though they did not exist. 'It has been most truly said that our land does not belong to us only,' said William Morris. 'It is not in any sense our property, to do as we like with it. We are only trustees for those that come after us.' To which I would add, 'and for our brothers and sisters here with us now'.

A century or two earlier, as a transgressor of property rights, my diary would surely have been packed with incident – if mantraps in the game coverts had not utterly deterred me from the start! Farms were worked by manpower, supplemented by slow, fourfooted horsepower. They were not the empty places they are now. By daylight I could never have escaped detection, and my success as a forager would have depended on whether the farmworkers saw me as friend or intruder. We would all have been interested in what the land had to offer us.

Then came Inclosure Acts, the legal process whereby common rights could be extinguished and land converted to freehold property. Now agricultural improvements could be made, but once land was inclosed, the next step was to enclose it, to keep stock from straying amongst the crops. For those who had relied on common land for sustenance, the Inclosure Acts fenced off the bounty and brought times of great hardship. Finally, cheap imported food and the Industrial Revolution deprived the agricultural worker of his job on the land and put him into a factory. The land emptied and the farm has become a bit like a factory too. There are hedgerows still where edible wild plants root in loamy soil, there are meadows which are grazed and grow lush, and the herb that nourishes the cow will sometimes nourish you. Crops grow where they have always grown, but the tilling, the sowing and the reaping are quick and mechanized. There are few workers on the farm, and when I did see other people usually they were ramblers.

What distinguished me from others who walked there? Ironically my own upbringing gives me more common ground with the landowner than the poacher. My father's origins were humble enough but he did well for himself and his children went to public schools. Along with my education went training to be a consumer of whatever my society saw fit to produce. By the time I came to write this book I was in my mid-forties running a small business concerned with photography and industrial publishing. There was nothing about my home or the standard of living we enjoyed in it to suggest the longing for self-sufficiency inside me. So the events and arguments here did not stem from necessity but from conviction.

For years I had thought of myself as a student of anarchy, believing that rules have a value, but that rulers have none. A youthful reluctance to conform failed to develop at the usual age for revolt, however, and I became first a journalist, latterly an entrepreneur. Still I studied anarchy, the works of Kropotkin, Bakunin, Tolstoy and my contemporaries Marcuse, Roszak and Goodman. For me the most famous phrase of anarchism, Proudhon's 'Property is theft' was a conceptual mine, an infinite source of reflection and debate.

In middle age I suddenly decided that something in my life should reflect what I believed. Whether the action was public or private was not at first important; I wanted to be true to myself rather than make a public exhibition of my principles. It is not important to me, even now, to make converts or receive approbation. It is enough for me that anyone of a like mind can be helped to recognize that they too have a choice of action. My field of action was Lockleys Farm.

Previously I had been simply a trespasser there, casually abandoning the approved path whenever my gaze and my interest strayed from it, returning to the footpath in due course and not much concerned whether I was required to straddle a fence or not, at the point of re-entry. We are commonly inhibited by the idea of 'trespass', somehow equating it with theft, but the two acts have little in common. Trespass is no crime, for in England everything is lawful unless expressly forbidden by Act of Parliament or common law. From trespass I progressed to foraging, and then to something more radical. I started a furtive kind of farming. Perhaps the countryside itself had affected me, or the seasons worked some kind of alchemy. But confronted with evidence that this piece of land could help to support me in addition to supporting its legal owner, the conviction grew that by accepting these natural resources I could connect with the seasonal life of the earliest settlers, and find something in the pattern of their lives that we have lost from ours.

If there is a single goal to be aimed for in life, I am not convinced that it always lies ahead. Perhaps it is hidden in the past. I did not try to live the neolithic life, to be exclusively a hunter-gatherer. To revert completely is to lose one's historical perspective. There is a continuity of life in every age which no experiment can duplicate, and all our actions are influenced in part by our ancestors, and by an awareness of those who will inherit what we leave. If I had been born in an earlier age I would have inherited a wealth of folk lore relating to subsistence, and would have been disciplined by a society which had in turn evolved on the basis of subsistence. I lacked this lore, but had instead some hindsight of how such societies fared. I made up for the lack of lore, as well as I could, through study, but experience proved the better teacher. I learned how to be a vagabond.

In the golden age of property, rich men feared the vagabond and passed savage laws to deter him. But the vagabond beat a path that all free men may follow. I took him as my exemplar because I sensed society's disapproval of initiatives like mine. At times I was stealthy, conscious of the embarrassment of confrontation by the farmer. It would have been easier to have retired to the library, to have dealt only with historical precedents or hypothetical infringements and to have argued a sterile case for all men to have access to all open land. But my convictions came through experience as well as through philosophizing. If I hadn't trespassed myself, I could never have been sure that the argument was not mere sophistry. So I explored the land fully, regardless of legal rights. I identified resources, and – first hesitantly, later boldly – I put these resources to good use.

Those who aspire to practise self-sufficiency strengthen themselves, however small a proportion of their own activities are devoted to this end and however much those activities are condemned by others as misguided or myopic. If you believe the society around you to be a distortion of what man could make it, at least you can prepare for change. This is what I attempted, somewhat in the manner of Gilbert White, who wrote to a friend:

> I shall make no apology for troubling you with the detail of a very simple piece of domestic economy, being satisfied that you think nothing beneath your attention that tends to utility . . .

All around me are the manifestations of technology. This book itself has first been composed on a typewriter, which I could not have made myself. It never seriously occurred to me to search for a quill and mix oak tannin with iron salts to make ink. Yet there is no necessity to be completely swamped by technology, and neo-Luddite that I am, I often wonder how life might be if we had not created an industrial society.

Our ancestors may have worked for a master, and have known what was his and what was theirs, but they knew also what the land could give them without a 'by your leave'. Sometimes the distinction was disputed. Out of these disputes over what came direct from the earth and what was the product of another man's enterprise, grew the concepts of common rights, of trespass and poaching.

Land has rarely to be restricted to one use only. A forest of oak trees planted for timber will also feed pigs on its acorns. A reservoir may be stocked with fish. A field of grain can be undersown to provide a bite for cattle after the harvest. By extending such co-operative enterprise a society could derive infinitely greater benefit from the land than we customarily do.

Because we make one use of land into an exclusive category, we have forgotten most of the free gifts which once formed a treasury of common rights and which are still available without prejudicing commercial usage. The conviction that common rights were a *right* and were not something that other men could bestow or curtail, came in time to change my life. Such rights carry with them a responsibility to respect the land

and not to deprive others of its bounty, whether they too are trespassers or landowners in fee simple. But providing I accept this responsibility I reject any move to restrain my enterprise.

Research in the library paralleled my foraging walks, however, the statute books revealing few outright prohibitions of my acts. Nor is it enough to say that if we were all trespassers life would be intolerable. It would be intolerable if everyone in this country drove to work, although they have every right to do so. Fortunately some still use public transport. The fact is that only a tiny proportion of the population is ready to accept the responsibility (others may see it as the risk) of trespassing, and the land can certainly absorb them without hazard to crops.

Looking back on the events described in this book, what surprises me most is the solitary nature of all the activities. This was *me*, just a few years ago before I accepted my own need for a more communal life. And yet what moved me to farm clandestinely moves me still, a need to explore ways of living off the land without owning it, without excluding the rights of others to have access to it.

The Clandestine Farm marked a transition period in my life. Today I grow crops more openly, but apart from my own garden I own none of the land on which they grow, I have no tenancy agreements, and instead of marauding rabbits I now lose a tithe of my harvest to vandals. I farm urban wasteland, and I work with others to make these disused plots productive. It is in material terms a more rewarding exercise and it no longer involves trespass because I farm with the approval and support of the landowners.

Our passion for parcelling and assigning land as property leaves many a neglected corner which is mine for the asking providing I expect no security. I gladly accept this impermanence, recognizing in these strips and allotments, gardens and churchyards, today's equivalent of the ancient manorial waste.

Not everyone who feels alienated from the land will want to go as far as I have gone. They may not understand why it is so important to take the gifts of the land; they may be concerned to know what the law permits, or to learn what difficulties they may encounter. It is to answer these questions that I have written this book.

I took a notebook and pencil with me on that first March walk, intending to record from that time on not only what I saw, and what I took from the farm, but also what happened to me, my adventures in avoiding the consequences of my aberrant behaviour. There are several volumes of that diary now, and I have drawn on them in part in writing this book. But what I failed to realize then, and which only came to me gradually a year or more later, was that becoming a trespasser was not a final solution, but the first stage in rejecting the structure on which my life until then had been based.

As my attitudes changed, so I found new interests, made new friends. Some had faced the tormenting decisions about jobs and family responsibilities which I was now forced to make. Others had never doubted the wisdom of rejecting conventional society's standards. Over and again I was to find an amused recognition of my predicament and to be told, at first to my alarm, later to my satisfaction, that 'there's no going back'. Although I had no inkling of it at first, out there, alone on the farm, I was taking part in a revolution.

If you become a clandestine farmer you will inevitably infringe some standards of behaviour which acquisitive societies adopt. While I defend the right of all individuals to experiment within the law, you should understand that persistent – or even occasional – trespass may invite the personal displeasure of landowners who, as a class, have always been inclined to take the law into their own hands. In law, every landowner or his tenant has a right to possession of his property undisturbed by trespassers, and the remedy for infringement of this private right is to sue the offender for damages in the civil court, or to apply there for an injunction against further trespass. The landowner who asks a trespasser to leave his land is within his rights, and the trespasser should leave by the shortest route. If he fails to do so immediately he cannot complain if minimal force is used to ensure compliance, though the landowner puts himself in the wrong if he uses more force than is necessary or deliberately causes injury.

As a clandestine farmer you should come in peace, and if asked, go in peace. Force destroys freedom. Avoid violence, avoid destruction. Close gates behind you, leave fences and walls undamaged. If you need to be reminded of any of the tenets of the Country Code, you are not yet ready for clandestine farming. For my part, I believed I was ready.

# 2 Lockleys Farm

My home is on a housing estate, intrusively grafted on a village which has lost its church, its manor house and half its agricultural land to the adjoining New Town of Welwyn Garden City. The front of the house is urban, but the back is rural. The neighbour at the bottom of my garden farms 400 acres.

You may have seen his land. Travel north by train from King's Cross on the Edinburgh express and within half an hour you pass Lockleys Farm. The first glimpse is from the viaduct, forty-one arches spanning the Mimram valley to provide a fair view of the southern slopes of the farm away ahead of you and to the west, where the fields slope from your horizon down to the river. A moment later you hurtle through Welwyn North station and into a tunnel. As you come briefly into the light again you can look up to a fringe of arable farmland between two woods, one of those timeless moments in a journey where your spirit might wish to cry halt. And then the next tunnel sucks the train and the spirit in and the vision is gone.

Beyond that summerline of swaying barley awns or overwintering furrowed fields is where I wandered.

Despite the setbacks I was later to suffer, I enjoyed my tenancy of the Clandestine Farm and the harvest I took from it. On a winter's night I relished my glass of elderberry wine. In the morning, preserved chestnut enriched homemade muesli. Wild strawberries are sweeter than any you can buy, and Jack-by-the-hedge is an excellent substitute for garlic in a salad. I munched salad burnet sandwiches when my last lettuce had bolted.

Wherever I look in my garden now, the surrounding land has supplemented what my own plot yields. Cabbages benefit from chalk dug from an outcrop and ground down for a soil dressing. The compost heap has a layer of gleaned straw (lifted before the farmer set fire to the field) between each layer of lawn mowings, to keep the ferment aired and sweet. The mortar in a brick wall I built is made of soil cement, which saved the cost of sand.

But these and many others were not benefits I reaped all at once. How could I find them when I had not really started looking? I had seen the farm in every season for ten years, but without really knowing it. Then came the time when the first radical seeds of this book were sown. I read *Walden* by Henry David Thoreau.

'Enjoy the land but own it not,' wrote Thoreau and threaded his life through with long contemplative walks in the New England forests which continued to nourish his spirit all his days. He wished to walk every day, and thought it no good news if a friend asked to join him. When I first read *Walden* I admired the manner in which the author lived off the land but was puzzled by what I thought of as an excessive delight in walking. In moderation, yes, but to patrol the ground repetitively seemed a restless use of time. Now I think otherwise. I believe that a walk in the country is a way to absorb inspiration, proportionate to our knowledge of what we encounter, and that the knowledge is the key to survival. The suspicion grew that any object, no matter how small, had the potential fascination of the universe, that travel over the globe might yield no more of value than would the perceptive, microscopic study of one acre – or perhaps even one cubic centimetre – of soil.

Such a close interest yields benefits at all levels. Philosophically it is invaluable, as William Blake knew –

> To see a World in a Grain of Sand,
> And a Heaven in a Wild Flower,
> Hold Infinity in the palm of your hand,
> And Eternity in an hour.

More particularly I hoped to learn how to improve crops of diverse wild foods, and all the time to derive simple enjoyment from the study. I came to rely on that pleasure, wanting to sense everything and appreciate the nature of every sensation, to permit each stimulus fair passage to my brain and to read the message whole. So the countryside exercised its magic on me, and I arrived at the place T. S. Eliot wrote of, the place from whence all my exploring began, and knew it for the first time. In my eyes this was no longer simply a farm, it was a portion of the earth, inseparable from it. Skim the surface with concrete and you blind a man's eye to the reality of the earth below, but here the earth was yielding its fruits undisguised.

So I saw each visit not as work, but as a walk. These fruitful walks brought with them all the pleasure, all the recreation found in a less purposeful ramble, and the joy of the activity overshadowed the disappointments. By its decentralized nature clandestine farming is inevitably linked with walking. When you recognize no boundaries to your field, why turn the furrow back on itself? So walking was both choice and necessity. 'I find it hard to understand how a philosopher can bring himself to travel in any other way,' wrote Rousseau; 'how he can tear himself from the study of the wealth which lies before his eyes and beneath his feet.' Whether a particular walk had a quickening effect on my mind, or whether the occasion was simply given up to a quiet appreciation of the life all around me, I always knew that the burden of cares and disagreements which might be with me when I started out, would fall as soon as I began to pace the farm footpaths.

You don't *have* to trespass to walk on Lockleys Farm, but even if you have a map, it is hard to avoid straying from the footpath; without a map it is virtually impossible. Few people walk there, though the ones who do are amply rewarded. 'Those only know a country who are acquainted with its footpaths,' wrote Richard Jefferies. 'By the roads indeed the outside may be seen; but the footpaths go through the heart of the land.'

Apart from the avenue leading straight to the farmhouse, the widest and firmest path is a bridleway which soon divides, one track leading to the back of the farm, and the other bisecting a field. Neither option is yours of right: both ways are private. You can, however, skirt the field, hugging the fringe of Puttockhill Wood, and eventually join up with Public Footpath No. 30, which runs roughly north and south. Even if you wish to tread circumspectly, the choice of direction is still a matter of indifference. Before you have walked a quarter of a mile in either direction, the path has ended and you are confronted either by ploughed field or growing crops, depending on the season. The country footpath map shows where you should walk, but rarely is the traffic sufficient to tread a path which is visible.

There is another approach. In the heart of Lockleys Wood a barely detectable path crosses the main route where it follows the line of the railway in the tunnel below. Once into the wood on this side path, the way is clear, and ahead you can see a gap, framed in hornbeam branches, with just two posts remaining of what was once a pretty stile. This is Footpath No. 38, traversing the whole farm from west to east. I compared Dury and Andrews's map of 1766 with the Ordnance Survey sheet and found the present path was shown by the early cartographers. It is a good grassed route through the fields, though sadly no hedge marks the way to help confirm its antiquity. But it is not all plain walking. As you climb the western rise of the farm you come to a stile in a field, and now you risk the insatiable curiosity and gelded aggression of bullocks, as they form up, charge, wheel and otherwise manoeuvre until your resolve to make a firm stand and return their hard looks, brings them to a halt, glowering, with horns lowered, just a few paces away. There is no visible path, but 200 yards ahead across oak-shaded pasture you will find another stile and a choice of ways by which to make your exit.

To enter the farm I usually grasped the branch of a tree which grew in my garden at the boundary, and swung myself over, clear of the barbed-wire strands below. Trees are not always so conveniently placed, however. A more handy formula is needed to deal with fences. As one of a party of beaters on the nearby Brocket Estate I once tried to emulate a young keeper who laid his walking stick on the wire and made this the fulcrum for his weight as his legs scissored over – but I was not so nimble. To cross a fence no more than crotch high you can grasp the wire with both hands, each cupping a barb, then swing a leg over using your hands as cushioning.

People who live conventional lives think that they are the disciplined ones, and that the transgressors lack moral fibre. But to the conformist, conforming is easy; it is breaking out which calls for special resolve. Once you are over the fence you are literally beyond the pale. The forager fears he is observed, the hunter suspects that he is the one who is hunted. Hedgerows may partly conceal you, but only the woodlands provide real sanctuary. You want to enter without causing a disturbance, which is like wanting to submerge yourself in a pool without rippling the surface. Inside the wood it is gloomy; the watcher concealed there sees one who approaches in silhouette. Growth luxuriates at the wood's edge and the forester leaves his loppings there as an obstacle even if there is no fence. Anxious not to be observed in the very act of entry you may find yourself bursting in, and arrive scratched, flustered and with thumping heart. The woodland creatures shrink away from the intruder. An autumn flock of roosting finches will rise in a chattering cloud, but pigeons may stay until you are under the tree which conceals them, and then make their preposterous wing-clapping exodus. The blackbird which had been scuffling in the dead leaves under a bush flies deep into the heart of the wood, its strident alarm call unreasonably prolonged, and when it is gone peace has been transformed into an ominous stillness.

These woods where I walked were derelict, but not deserted. The farmer had leased them to the Forestry Commission, whose ranger occasionally brought retribution to muntjac deer which damaged the trees. Another sportsman concealed himself here by arrangement with the farmer to await the roosting pigeons and sell them to the butcher to pay for his cartridges. He set out decoys in the fields, or walked the woods putting up birds as he went. I didn't want to meet either of these sanctioned hunters, and so I walked circumspectly.

The old scout lore I resurrected dealt with tracking Boers on the veldt, and detecting the spoor of game. I worked out my own rules for stealthy traverse of an English woodland. Pause at the first line of trees and await the return of peace instead of that unreal silence. The sibilant gossip of bluetits or goldcrests in the treetops as they resume their hunt for food may be the first identifiable sound, but before that there is an intangible relaxing of tension which may only have been in your mind – or the pounding of your heart.

The summer canopy of leaves forms an umbrella over the thickets to keep them dry. Dead branches become brittle, and brushwood may snap if you bend it. To move stealthily, part the green branches that impede you, but avoid the dry ones completely. Watch where you place your feet; there may well be deadwood which you can't see, but if it is buried it is more likely to have rotted to softness than the surface debris has. Choose grassed or mossy rides for your route rather than crunching through leaf litter. The more damp underfoot, the softer the footfall. For real stalking have the sun behind you and the wind in your face: that way you see and hear before you are seen and heard. Pause frequently and listen. You won't be able to avoid making some noise, but if you can break the regular pattern of footsteps there is more chance that the custodian of the woods will fail to recognize the origin of the sounds as human.

When you are on the move the pigeon, the blackbird and the pheasant may give your presence away, but once you are settled on some foraging or farming task they will keep watch for you. Don't ignore their warnings if you want your presence to remain a secret. Leave your coat and haversack behind a bush and be prepared to join them for a while until the coast is clear once more.

What I first sought from the woods and fields was food, and if everything green were good to eat I would have had no shortage, for a rich profusion of plants grew wherever the farmer and the forester had left a space. The farmer decreed barley, but up sprang wild oats and field bindweed too. The forester of an earlier century planned hornbeam coppice, but between and beneath the trees a million bluebells were stirring from dormancy. These wild plants were what the earth was offering me. I had always loved to see them; now I wanted to consume them too. But which? I turned to books for advice.

The limitation of the printed page as a source of knowledge is never more apparent than when a beginner naturalist is studying his guide to wild flowers. Everything he needs to effect an identification is there, but the detail overwhelms and confuses. When I started to walk in hornbeam woods in the spring, acquisitively eyeing every green shoot as a potential potherb, the lack of flowers was a constant frustration. And when the dog's mercury which carpets the coppiced woodland in many places eventually produced a flower which was itself green I confessed myself utterly baffled and took a wilted specimen round to a botanist friend. He identified it for me, but only after some reflection and a quick look at his Clapham, Tutin and Warburg.

The hesitation was natural. In the woodland glade where I had picked the plant he could have named it at once. The plant itself provided some of the clues, but almost as valuable were those denied him: the situation, the associated vegetation – even the date when the plant was picked could be important. Emerson wrote of Thoreau that if he 'waked up from a trance ... he could tell by the plants what time of the year it was within two days'. Where plants clothe the landscape it is always changing, but just as the situation helps to identify the plants, so do the plants tell a great deal about the situation, about its climate and geology. Knowledge of these facts is vital to the clandestine farmer if he is to avoid making allies of plants that are really misfits.

My disappointment at not being able to name dog's mercury unaided was increased when I discovered that the plant was poisonous. Here I was, in the still dormant woods where old man's beard climbed hemp-stemmed over gaunt trees, its flowers a weathered white display like sheep's wool teased out on a wire fence, and almost everything was dead and dried and unappetizing save this abundant ground covering of *Mercurialis perennis*. And it could not be eaten. I returned home, a frustrated forager.

Progress was slow. I see now that my gradual appreciation of what the woods could offer me was held in check by concern for my well-being and for those who might share my meals. I never allowed myself to become complacent, but I did grow more confident in my judgments on what was fit to eat and what best avoided. An early volume, well thumbed, was *Poisonous Plants* and when I started on fungi each specimen was subjected to a double check. First, what plant do I believe this to be? Second, is there any plant listed as poisonous that even remotely resembles it? If the answer to the second question was yes, I went through every identification mark until I could positively eliminate the specimen from the list of the toxic or unwholesome. If I could not, I discarded it.

Foraging whets all the senses, but perhaps the sense of taste is the more important. Certainly it improves your chances of surviving the game of dietary roulette, because some of the deadlier plants have an unpleasant taste or smell. But the wider your browsing extends, the greater the chance of encountering one of the few poisonous plants, so accurate identification is vital.

While I have been writing this book, my own patterns of browsing have changed. Some species which initially attracted me, I now shun. I have good recipes for 'fiddlehead greens' and the young bracken shoots necessary to prepare the dishes are certainly there in abundance on the farm, but I am not inclined to consume a plant which has been labelled a cancer risk. There is a Suffolk legend of how a starving populace was saved from famine by the sea pea, which still fruits deliciously on the shingle foreshore, and I asked Richard Mabey how he came to omit it from *Food for Free*. He said he believed it to be another suspect species. Even that much recommended self-sufficiency vegetable, chickweed, contains a poisonous substance called saponin, and should not be made a staple item in anyone's diet.

Closely allied to a keen sense of taste is that of smell, possession of which helps in positive identification of many herbs; to savour the mild garlic aroma released from a leaf of Jack-by-the-hedge when rolled between the fingers, to identify wild thyme at a sniff and to know fennel for sure because it is redolent of aniseed, these are all forms of knowledge which bring a fresh dimension to a country walk.

Throughout April the spring flowers bloomed in sequence, so that each walk yielded a new species. Some early bluebells on the high woodland over the railway tunnels, golden celandine, violets and wood anemones 'constant to their early time', all racing the onset of the summer foliage which would steal their light. But as the cuckoo arrived at the month's end and flowering accelerated beyond my willingness to botanize, identify and list, I cherished the appearance of scores of cowslip clumps on the Bottom Park meadow and treated all else as frame, easel and canvas to a work of art. Tempt me not with recipes for cowslip wine, I would not have the fate of one plant on my conscience.

The evenings can be so good in all spring weathers – once the showers have lost their chill sting. I walked in rain up to the hawthorn spinney, lately the winter haunt of fieldfare and redwing, now a place to stand concealed and watch young swallows hunting cow-high over the pasture. While I watched I sensed rather than saw the cock pheasant concealed in a clump of grass, and crept within two feet of him before he blasted off, voiding excrement like ballast abandoned in panic. Two muntjac deer had chosen the half-light time to leave the shelter of Puttockhill Wood and graze a hundred yards from my cover.

Despite my frustrated desire to feed from nature's larder, there were many such consolations; but I felt a common bond with those pale ancestors who had to survive this time of premature flowering, the 'hungry gap' when winter's stores were gone, and all were on short commons. By the following year I had at this stage of the calendar eaten young nettle shoots, hawthorn buds and the first new leaves of the dandelion with scarcely a hint of bitterness, but it was chickweed that first filled my food bowl that year, and I deemed it excellent.

The diary record is valuable, because plant appearance can be deceptive and most greens have their off season. In October that year I worked as cook-for-the-day in a Welsh commune and wrestled for hours with bowls of chickweed to be second vegetable for twelve, only to find that by the autumn it is tough instead of succulently tasty, and the plant tips alone should be picked.

I used Richard Mabey's recipe:

> Wash the sprigs well, and put into a saucepan without any additional water. Add a knob of butter, seasoning, and some chopped spring onions. Simmer gently for about ten minutes, turning all the time. Finish off with a dash of lemon juice or a sprinkling of grated nutmeg.

Chickweed, prolific in most gardens, is a good green vegetable, unlike so many of the wild larder items which are mere garnishes or flavourings to some conventional fare.

While I was prepared to sample and enjoy as many as possible of the 300 or so edible wild plants that grow in this country, what primarily exercised my mind was the source of sustaining foods, energy-rich and body-building, prolific in growth, the basis of economic foraging. While tuning to the seasons I tried to catch the food supply at its peak within each plant.

It is likely that early man found the inner bark of trees served as a useful staple food, when the trees outnumbered him and handicapped his horticulture. If your landscape is entirely wooded, and deforestation is your life work, it's no bad thing to ring a few birch or elms, to strip the sap-rich phloem layer from under the bark and consume it. But I felt I had to wait until a more compelling reason arose to fell a suitable tree and sample this food.

The rising sap springs the leaf, and with the year's advance I would expect to find the green parts of the plant, then its flower and finally its fruit would yield the most sustaining portion, until autumn caused the plant to die back and the root became its stock until another spring.

Early growth has an urgency about it that rattles the dead brown calm of the woods. I saw a bundle of leaf mould thrust through by the fast emerging leaves of bluebells and speared incongruously aloft. The farmer sensed that urgency too and began spraying 'Milfaron' fungicide and 'Bidisin' selective herbicide to give his wheat and barley a head start.

No longer was it a question of sampling wildings on their own. Now I had a choice and could orchestrate the flavours. But I lacked experience. Improvisation in the kitchen is as rare as on the stage or in the concert hall. Most cooks rely on their script, their score – the recipe, which requires fixed proportions of ingredients to set off the main constituent of the dish. It is not always possible to use recipes with garnered foods, for they never grow to order. I tried to learn the flavour of a new plant, but went on to experiment with salads which would accommodate whatever I could find and introduce a diversity of flavours.

It didn't always work out as I hoped. From my notebook: 'Cold meat for supper. Made a salad from lettuce with dandelion leaves, salad burnet, fennel and Jack-by-the-hedge, with salt, pepper, oil and cider vinegar. Pretty vile. Too many tastes conflicting and I suspect old dandelion leaves were bitter. Lesson: proceed by simple combinations to the more complex.'

Two weeks later I was using just salad burnet and Jack-by-the-hedge as salad supplements, and was pleased with the result.

Even if the combination of tastes is not actually offensive, it can result in a loss of character: the cook's repertoire of flavours is much like the artist's palette, where the more colours you mix, the greyer the result. Certainly, I was making mistakes and was to make many more. But I was learning.

# 3 Forgive us our trespasses

On 29 May I set out on a cold wet walk to the junction of Footpath 30 and Footpath 38 to re-establish the ploughed-up path. The cowslips on the bank had come to the end of their month of blossom and hung sadly, withering and colourless. On the ground and in the hedge flanking Lockleys Wood there was a long 'burn' of brown vegetation which looked like the result of a chemical spray. When I reached the main footpath where it emerged from the wood I turned and walked downhill.

Three hundred yards from the woodland crossroads where the path began, it should have been joined by Footpath 30, but 100 yards of green flowed without interruption between where I stood and the southernmost tip of Foxley Grove – the nearest point at which the path was visible. I turned in to the field of corn which stood higher than my knees and headed north to make the link-up.

In one respect it was a painful act, trampling into the soil these young shoots of barley. Rights did not come into it. In my ideology the fact that someone else had planted seed in the ground to cultivate a crop extinguished the rights of passage at least temporarily until the harvest was over. So why, if it pained me, did I walk wide, scuffling a broader passage than my own journey justified, bending twice as many plants as the minimum number I might have crushed? I did it in the interest of the survivors. Logic told me that these few plants would comprise an infinitely small proportion of the total crop, and a negligible part too of the plants that would be lost through pigeon consumption, fungus spoilage, and storm damage. My aim therefore was to establish by this crossing, the summer's course of Footpath 30, so that others might not pioneer new paths, as they unwittingly would if mine was not well defined. The field was immense, a detour was out of the question.

The theory was sound, but the execution was less than effective, though I reached Foxley Grove with my trousers soaked from rampaging through the rain-sodden crop. For many weeks after this, although I walked it regularly, the path remained almost indistinguishable from the pattern of planting determined by the seed drill, and through the summer I often found myself in doubt as to which way I should turn, as I ran the gauntlet of the loaded heads of grain, which seemed to strike at my legs vindictively for my presumption in crossing a field of crops.

Although technically at fault, the farmer has to plan cultivation within the limits of mechanical help. To turn the tractor back short of the footpath, to divide the field into two when he sowed the barley, would be wasteful of time, fuel, effort – and land. I happily accept the responsibility of reaffirming my rights as a walker, but if I'm criticized for doing it, I'll shelter under the Highways Act 1959 Section 119 and the Countryside Act 1968 Section 28, and say that by law it was the farmer's duty to reinstate the path.

It may seem that I am on shaky ground calling the law to my defence, when my thesis concerns trespass, but the law supports me. If you doubt this, consult Stone's *Justices' Manual* which states, ' "Trespassers will be prosecuted" is a threat as empty as ever it was, unless actual damage is committed.'

I advise my children to treat with contempt such notices which seek to deter them from crossing a boundary. There's no such notice on Lockleys Farm. Am I prepared then to have strangers climb my fence and wander at will in my garden? I grant you, I would be less than happy if I found them doing so, for my garden is restricted enough to be almost entirely in view of my home, and to be in regular use for the modest pleasure of my family. If my land were so extensive that strangers could trespass without encroaching on my privacy, I would not object. I would certainly not introduce checks and traps to deter them providing they caused no damage. So when *I* trespass I do so with discretion.

The courts' power to deal with the invasion of private property has been well gauged by the reaction to urban squatting. Where entry has been effected by a ruse rather than by forcing a window or door, and where the property has been vacated without damage to structure or content, the squatters have escaped without incurring any penalty. Their leaders have carefully studied the rules to see how far they can go in seeking moral justice for the homeless in the world that only enforces legal justice, and they believe that the greatest danger is to be charged with 'conspiracy to trespass and unlawful assembly'.

My trespasses are solitary, and therefore I cannot be accused of conspiracy (although you never know, bearing in mind the occasion when William Cobbett was approached by an under sheriff 'telling me to disperse or he would take me into custody!' If a man on his own can be asked to disperse, perhaps he can also conspire!). But what I might more likely fall foul of is a charge of persistent trespass. Providing my detected lapses are only occasional, I feel that I can wriggle through that mesh of the legal net, too.

It is reasonable to consider the risks others might run if a landowner strenuously opposed them through the courts. Under a statute of 1381 it is an offence to enter into land or tenements 'with strong hand or multitude of people', but to be charged under this Forcible Entry Act it would be necessary to prove that you intended to claim the land and remain in possession of it. As trespass is itself a civil offence, the landowner's only redress for actual or imagined damage would be through action in civil court.

You may think that if you trespass in the country and return home with a basket of edible fungi, salad plants, nuts, fruit and herbs picked from private land, that you will have caused damage by removing private property. But this is not the case, as Stone's *Justices' Manual* explains, describing the concept of property in the Criminal Damage Act of 1971:

> In this Act 'property' means property of a tangible nature, whether real or personal, including money and (a) including wild creatures which have been tamed or are ordinarily kept in captivity, and any other wild creatures or their carcasses if, but only if, they have been reduced into possession which has not been lost or abandoned or are in the course of being reduced into possession, but (b) not including mushrooms growing wild on any land or flowers, fruit or foliage of a plant growing wild on any land. For the purposes of this subsection 'mushrooms' includes any fungus and 'plant' includes any shrub or tree.

It was not until my first year of clandestine farming was well advanced and I was fully into the spirit of the game that a new concern beset me. Taken to its logical conclusion, clandestine farming made possible the gypsy life, and brought in train the opprobrium which attaches to travelling people in western eyes. Here was a potential catalyst for harassment.

Moriaty's *Police Law* says that the Vagrancy Act of 1824 was intended to prevent wasters and sturdy beggars from wandering about the country and committing sundry questionable acts by which an easy livelihood might be gained. Just reading it is enough to make me blush. The Vagrancy Act of 1935 gives the police power to arrest without warrant any person wandering abroad and lodging in any barn or outhouse or unoccupied dwelling or in the open air or under a tent or any cart or wagon (with or in which he does not travel) and not giving a good account of him/herself, provided that he declines any reasonably accessible free place of shelter, or that he is a person who persistently wanders abroad and sleeps out, or that by so sleeping out he causes or appears to cause damage, infection with vermin or other offensive consequences to property.

To be found guilty of these 'offences' is to risk punishment as a rogue and vagabond, with imprisonment for a term between fourteen days and three months, and a fine of £25. For a second offence imprisonment may be for up to twelve months, and the offender is termed an incorrigible rogue. Under the same Act, any citizen may arrest one who is 'found on premises or found wandering' or who is found 'frequenting and loitering'.

What concerns me is the imprecision of terms such as 'giving a good account of oneself', 'causing or appearing to cause damage' and 'found wandering'. From being an academic exercise, study of the law suddenly took on a new importance as I saw a theoretical threat to my freedom. Was it conceivable that my actions could bring me before the magistrates?

On one walk I daydreamed, conducting a spirited defence without the aid of counsel, sending up legal parlance to the best of my ability, along these lines: 'On a point of law, m'lud, I crave your indulgence. Moriaty is quite clear in the matter of vagrancy, but all things are changed and we with them, as the Emperor said, *Tempora mutantur, nos et mutamur in illis*. The consensus in society today is less rigid, and far from believing unquestioningly that man's work is a calling, men are remembering Christ's sermon on the Mount; and consider the lilies of the field who toil not, neither do they spin. The work that one man is paid to do may be in the worst interests of society, while another who has no job may shine with God's grace through the spiritual value of his life's work. And who will say that independence is to be scorned?'

I was not alone in feeling that these laws were out of date, a punitive hangover from a past age when attitudes were prevalent which are unacceptable in a Welfare State. Consequently, in 1971 a working party was appointed by Mr Reginald Maudling 'to consider the law relating to vagrancy and other street offences', and a working paper was published in 1974. The authors note that the vagrancy laws were designed to deal with very different social conditions from those of the present day, and as an example observe that 'it is clear that not everyone who sleeps rough is necessarily a vagrant, that is to say, a destitute wanderer'. Vagrancy only carries a stigma when night falls. It is the lack of a fixed abode which troubles society, as it did the old lawmakers.

In the wider context of international morality, trespass may be tolerated, provided the trespasser is big enough. The thinly veiled aggression within the political arena reminds me of the story retold by John Seymour, of the large tramp who went to sleep in a field and woke to find a small squire standing over him, ordering him out. The tramp said: 'How did you get this field?' The squire said: 'I got it from my ancestors.' 'How did they get it?' 'They fought for it.' 'Right,' said the tramp taking his coat off. 'I'll fight you for it.'

Despite our obsession with the concept of property rights, we are not slow to claim use of common resources if it is in our interest. When the Welsh National Water Development Authority decided to ask for an additional payment in respect of the millions of gallons they export to England, they got short shrift from the Severn-Trent Water Authority chairman, Sir William Dugdale. 'We are wholeheartedly against paying any form of profit,' he was reported as saying. 'The water falls from heaven and belongs to the nation as a whole.'

In the larger amphitheatre of oil politics there appear to be those who are saying that oil gushes out of the underworld and belongs to the world as a whole – an argument which appeals to me, but comes gratingly from a spokesman of a nation built on the acquisitiveness of private enterprise. The *Daily Telegraph* reported on 3 January 1975 that Dr Henry Kissinger, then American Secretary of State, declined to rule out American military action in the Middle East if Arab oil policies were seen to be causing 'a strangulation of the industrialized world'. Some time later an article in the *Observer* told of an off-the-record briefing to American newsmen in which Dr Kissinger confessed he had not been serious. But to be able to bluff with conviction your adversary must see that you have no cultural restraints against such international aggression, however much you may choose to curb it.

Attitudes towards acts of trespass are conditioned by the current system of land tenure, and today's freehold owner assumes total jurisdiction. It is a principle of English law that no land can be unowned, yet of the several million acres of common land existing at the time of the Norman Conquest, there still remain 1.5 million acres, a little over 4 per cent of the total land surface of England and Wales. But the status of common land has changed over the centuries. Once it would have been common property; today it is private property, subject to certain rights over its surface.

The feudal practice of the lord loaning land to the village became universal with the completion of the Domesday Book in 1086. After the Conquest, William I parcelled up the land of the country amongst his followers, who became his tenants for their land, holding by his grant. The tenure thus created was knight-service. The families who actually wrested the agricultural wealth of the country from the soil were not evicted; they were bound by service to the lord to perform various public duties, such as repairing bridges, providing food, or working on the lord's crops as well as their own. Service was the original form of rent: scutage (or shield rent) in which the tenant served in the lord's army; frankalmoign, involving spiritual services such as praying for the souls of the grantor and his ancestors; or the simple socage, calling for service labouring in the fields. The range of medieval tenures is enormous and included the provision of a hangman or executioner, the supply of straw for the royal privy, or the holding of the seasick king's head on channel crossings! In time virtually all were commuted to cash rents.

What is clear, though, is that however firm the hold a lord had over his tenants, they retained the use of the land. Only the *king* owned it. On this basis, whatever the ramification of land law today, I maintain that the freehold occupier has full use of his land, but not exclusive use. Others must have access to land as much as to air and sunlight. However much of an ass the law has become, it wisely leaves prosecutions for trespass to the civil courts. If trespass should become a crime, we are lost.

In seeking resources from land owned by another, it is not necessary always to enter the land oneself. Precedents for trespass by proxy extend back to the earliest medieval dovecots, when the consumption of squabs gave the lord some meat during the winter after the last of the cattle feed had gone. It was always the young offspring of the doves which were eaten, for the parent birds mate for life and were therefore spared. The crops of the villager, however, were *not* spared, and the trespass by doves on their holdings constituted as effective a theft of their produce as if the lord himself had strode down and stripped the rows. Today we steal from our neighbours with impunity if we keep bees, although the theft is of a resource that would otherwise be wasted – nectar – and the bees provide a reciprocal service in pollinating the gardener's flowering vegetables and fruit trees. Not so attractive is the trespass by pollution, whether of bonfire smoke or the more insidious noise pollution inflicted by a radio or television at high volume, or the high-altitude cacophony directed at those whose homes lie below busy aircraft flight paths. When solar collectors become a commonplace fitment on roofs, to allow buildings or trees to overshadow them may be deemed a trespass, a latterday infringement of Ancient Lights. None of us is immune to trespass, but if the invasion is discreet and steals nothing which we count a loss, where is the harm, compared with the loss of peace, or light, or clean air? 'I wonder (upon my soul I do),' wrote William Cobbett, 'that there is no lawyer, Scotchman, or Parson-Justice, to propose a law to punish the rooks for *trespass*.'

Owners are naturally suspicious when their land is invaded, but invariably I have a pair of binoculars around my neck and am dismissed as a harmless birdwatcher. Birdwatching is perhaps the most widely tolerated of the Englishman's idiosyncrasies, and I not only practise it but use the glasses to spot nuts on a tree or mushrooms in a field. I recommend the disguise!

On farmland the trespasser may fare well. On estates, particularly those supporting a syndicate of sportsmen, a more feudal situation prevails. I have been warned off an immense Yorkshire moorland estate because I might disturb the grouse, and the wiles of landholders and their gamekeepers in preventing access are notorious, even where footpaths exist. On one Midlands estate a gamekeeper told me of the fear expressed by His Lordship that some day an existing right of way through his game coverts might be signposted by the County Council. Meanwhile the two of them conspired to perpetuate the myth that no footpath rights existed, and the keeper maintained three strands of barbed wire stretched across a strategic gap. This is how he described to me what happened next:

'I saw a party of ramblers once coming up the hill on the path and lay in wait for them until they were half-way across a field. Then I showed myself and asked them where they were going. They said they were walking the footpath. "Oh yes?" says I. "Well, tell me this. How wide is a footpath?" They didn't know. "I'll tell you," I said. "It's three feet wide. And look at you, all strung out across the field. You can't all be on it. You'd better get into single file." So they did, and we all walked on together until we reached the wired-off gap. Then I said to them, "If this is a footpath as you claim, tell me exactly where it goes after this." There was no sign of a path, and naturally they didn't know its course, so I sent them packing and we never saw them again.'

In earlier days there was nothing like this rigidity regarding land access. Even where no common rights existed, it was customary to open the fields to the villagers once the harvest was in, so they could graze their cattle on the stubble until Candlemas, when the new crop was due to be planted. Both parties benefited from this practice, the owner having his land manured.

Now that few of us have livestock to graze, it may be more useful to consider instead the practice of gleaning ears of corn which had inevitably been dropped by the workers at harvest time, and are still dropped by the combine harvester. In Biblical times there was a strong element of charity about the practice by which villagers gathered the grain which the reapers had failed to remove, or the grapes which remained after the vintage, and the custom was well established in the English countryside right up until the end of the nineteenth century, but by then it was only considered worth the effort if times were hard.

In Hertfordshire in the 1890s some twenty parishes still rang 'gleaners' bells' at harvest time. Though the bells no longer sound, the mighty combine does not suck up all of the grain. R. K. Murton has said that 100 acres of stubble will feed 154 pigeons (the average post-breeding population for such an area) for twenty-six weeks. His estimate is that 3 per cent of the wheat and 6 per cent of barley grains are shed on the ground by the combine and lost at harvest time. If I kept chickens I'd send them to glean on my behalf.

Neglected lands – before the age of Inclosures – gave the peasant class the chance to live, even if life was frugal. The empty lands of today offer new opportunity, though our population is too great now for self-sufficiency to be universal. The benefits are much the same as they were hundreds of years ago.

The cottages who hauled home a sledgeful of kindling or turves for the fire were no vagabonds; but the free produce of the countryside attracted a special kind of individual who strayed to the limits of legal enterprise and who would rather spend all day foraging along the hedges than labour for one hour at the farm. Such a man was the moucher, whose calendar was recorded faithfully by Richard Jefferies.

In January he would be out with his billhook cutting briar stocks for grafting. He collected moss for flower pots, and used a decoy bird as he went fowling for linnets. The townsman's cage bird provided the market for his February harvest of snail shells and turves for its cage. By March he might have taken a wage driving cattle, but he was also trapping lizards as pets and making up bundles of primroses, violets and ferns to sell to the ladies. Nor was he averse to stealing turnip tops throughout the spring, to sell them. Watercress was the April crop, and more fowling for chaffinches, and their nests and eggs.

Summer was the moucher's busiest season, gathering dandelion leaves, parsley, sow thistle and clover to feed rabbits in the towns; worms, grubs and flies as fishing bait; quaking grass as an ornament; and enough creatures to stock a pet shop: goldfinch, linnets, young rabbits, squirrels, harvest mice, snakes. Then to round off the autumn, he would be away after mushrooms, blackberries, elderberries and sloes.

The moucher was a trader; he practised a cash economy which the cottager did not. Perhaps he was the first entrepreneur. But he, along with the poacher, and particularly the town-based poaching gang which came out in force to take game, attracted the attention of the gamekeeper and queered the pitch for everyone else. Catch-the-trespasser became a country game, sometimes lighthearted, sometimes deadly serious.

Jefferies describes the gamekeeper on his rounds, acting the part of both player and umpire.

> Suddenly he pauses in his walk, stoops, and points out to me in the grass the white, smooth, round knob-like tops of several young mushrooms which are pushing their way up. He carefully covers these with some pieces of dead bark and desiccated dung, so that none of 'them lurching fellows as comes round shan't see 'em' – ? with a wink at his own cunning – so as to preserve them until they have grown larger.

But mouchers and lurchers are only a step from gypsies and vagrants in their manner, and all are potentially riflers of the sportsman's yard. The gamekeeper tightens his resolve.

> He is like a spider in the centre of a vast spreading web, and the instant the most outlying threads – in this case represented by fences – are broken, he is all agitation till he has expelled the intruder. Men and boys in the winter come stealing into the wood where the blackthorn thickets are, for sloes, which are reputed to be improved by the first frosts, and are used for making sloe gin. Those they gather, they sell, of course; and although the pursuit may be perfectly harmless in itself, how is the keeper to be certain that, if opportunity offered, these gentry would not pounce upon a rabbit or anything else?

Freedom to roam the countryside and avail ourselves of its resources may lead to licence, when freedom for the many is imperilled by the acts of a few – but I am not here as advocate for my fellow man. We will learn to live in harmony when we have acquired respect for ourselves, for our neighbours and for the land. The man who spoils my world through greed has not proved the case for exclusive property rights, but only confirmed that he is not ready for freedom. Society offers chains in plenty for those who need them. I prefer to leave the shackles for others.

# 4 Private land and common rights

However safe I was legally, throughout my first year of clandestine farming I played a cat-and-mouse game, and was never in doubt who was the mouse. Nor did I doubt that my radical views would be anathema to George Baron of Lockleys Farm. Property was his creed.

Oddly enough, it was he who trespassed first on me – or at least, his pigs did – one autumn afternoon when one of his sows had been left to lead her litter on a tour of the farm to root for acorns under any oak tree they could find. The farm fence kept the sow under control, but the piglets ran into my garden, and that was where George Baron found them, dancing and snuffling around in the leaf layer. I have a photograph of George, stick threateningly raised in the classic 'Get off my land!' posture of the landowner, but it was actually the pigs he was chasing, and he was herding them back on to the field!

The manor house of Lockleys was built at the lowest part of the estate, down by the Mimram with the old Great North Road passing its door, but the farmhouse stands exposed on the hill. One evening I walked up there to spend an hour or two with George Baron, sitting across the parlour from him, half smothered in a deep chintz-covered armchair, with a glass of whisky in my hand. It was a strange situation, legal owner entertaining interloper, and I did not confess the usufructuary rights I had claimed.

'I've been asked to sell this farm, but I'll never part with it, not a bit of it,' he tells me. 'But what will become of it after I've gone?' I think it prudent not to mention my theory of land stewardship. A farm like this would naturally go to the first son, but George Baron had only daughters.

On the wall there is a pretty watercolour of an ivy-covered farmhouse. He tells me that we are seated in it now, although it looks so different. 'A stoat ran across the window sill and frightened my wife so much I cut all the ivy down.'

He says that he has entertained a Russian ambassador in this very room, all on account of his pedigree saddleback pigs. 'I've had a lot of fun with pigs in my time. I don't know how many firsts I've had. Five firsts at Blackpool Royal. That was a good touch, that was. Fifteen of my pigs went to the Seychelles last year. Japan, Italy, Brazil. I sold six gilts to Russia. That was when the ambassador came here from London. They were straight, I thought I'd get some more trade, but I never heard another line. One of the gilts won the championship at the Moscow State Fair.'

A man of the land, he keeps a prudent eye on all his 400 acres, sees when a fence needs mending, knows when a crop is prime for harvesting, notes the little muntjac deer in his garden when he rises – always at 6.30 – and hears the tawny owl when he goes to bed at half past ten. A man of fixed habit; when a bill comes in the morning post, his cheque goes off in the afternoon. But discipline and habit haven't walled him off like a business farmer in a counting house where all is output per man-hour, profit per bushel. He knew when the vixen moved her litter to a new lair in the woods; he can show you where the badger's sett is now.

He sees me trespass, but like most farmers he senses who comes in understanding of the land, and who does not. It is not vandalism that poses the real threat to the farmer, merely ignorance, and the man who stands and looks, who stands his ground too and looks the farmer in the eye when he is asked his business, and talks to the farmer – such a one may be welcome. I was never asked to leave.

I have resurrected the former rights of all commoners, but I have no evidence of a time when Digswell had a common, or any stretch of manorial waste. Hertfordshire has always been as William Camden described it, the county with 'the most footsteps of antiquity', and early use meant early abuse. There are no inclosure maps for Digswell because the land was effectively inclosed for the lord of the manor before the pressure for land improvement began.

Lockleys Farm lies on the ecclesiastical parish boundary dividing Welwyn from Digswell, a wooded area to the north of the

Mimram which from Norman times provided 'warren' for Digswell's manor lords – warren being the hunting of the small beasts of the chase. My own home in Digswell is in Warren Way, and the trees in the garden are the indigenous species of mid-Hertfordshire: hornbeam, oak, a sprinkling of ash, cherry and silver birch, the kinds of tree which were here long before those thirty-seven men and their families who are recorded in the Domesday Book of 1086.

By 1274 one Laurence de St Michael had free warren on one side of the river and claimed it on the other side too, along with 'view of frankpledge, gallows, and amend of the assize of bread and ale'. He obtained a charter from Henry III to hold a market every week on a Thursday, and an annual fair lasting ten days beginning on the vigil of St John the Evangelist.

By 1415 there are records of a manor at Lockleys when reversion of tithes is obtained for the three sons of John Peryent. It was May and just three weeks since the death of John's wife, Joan. Nikolaus Pevsner observed the 'outstandingly fine brasses to John Peryent, Standard Bearer to Richard II, and his wife' in the little church of St John the Evangelist. When you roll back the carpet which protects them you can see a hedgehog nestling at the feet of the knight's lady.

Another century passes and we have a map of part of the Lockleys estate, which shows also a vineyard in Digswell. The oldest artefact on the farm today is the big barn, which dates, George claims, from 1684. There is farming on the estate by then, but it is still as it always was, primarily a pleasure park. The records of owners become more comprehensive. In 1749 Richard Serle is at Lockleys. When Dury and Andrews drew their map in 1766, Charles Gardener Esquire is the owner. By the middle of the nineteenth century Lockleys is the home of a man who was squire, inventor and eccentric all in one: George Dering.

There are many local tales about Dering and many must be apocryphal, but his inventive skills are undisputed, and in the opinion of local historian Branch Johnson 'could not have failed to earn a place in technological history had circumstances compelled him to greater activity in exploiting his patented inventions'. Dering established a gasworks in Welwyn in 1860 – a very early date for a village to have one – and lit the streets first of Welwyn, then Codicote, Digswell and Tewin Water. He invented a fishplate for use on the railway. And he had the wealth to tend Lockleys as it had never been tended before.

The mallard swim on a tiny pond at the top of the hill, just in front of Lockleys farmhouse, concealed by trees. This was the reservoir for Dering's hydraulic fountain in front of his house.

'They tell me it was a five-inch pipe made of lead,' says George Baron, looking out of his window at the pond. 'Be worth something today if you dug that up.' He likes to talk about Dering, although, as he says, 'I never saw him. My grandmother saw him. Granny was 101 when she died. Good old girl. Real Christian.'

Dering's bailiff lived at the farm in those days. 'There were twenty-five gardeners and George Bennett was the foreman.'

Welwyn has been linked with many celebrities. A commanding position on the old Great North Road only a day's ride from London made this inevitable. Pepys spent the night at the Wellington in 1664, and it is said that Dr Johnson took tea there in 1781. George Baron says he remembers Mrs Pankhurst coming in her day, but the strangest visitor must surely have been Charles Blondin who became world-famous when he crossed the Niagara Falls on a tightrope. He stayed at Lockleys and carried George Dering across the Mimram, wheeling him in a barrow along the tightrope! That rope hangs still in the old barn, one of George Baron's most treasured possessions.

George was born in 1893 in the butcher's shop in Welwyn. When he was fifteen his father gave up the butcher's business and went to Lince's Farm, which now belongs to George's brother Donald. In 1922 George – who had been a tenant at Manor Farm, Ayot – acquired a lease of Lockleys Farm and in 1953 he bought the freehold. He made a farm of it. Dering died in 1911 and his house is now a school.

'In 1912 there was one big park here,' says George Baron. 'Sir Evelyn and Lady de la Rue took the mansion after Dering died. They used to let the shoot to people. Mr and Mrs Dewar from over at Danesbury had the shooting for some time. Then a Mr Cohen had it for two years . . .'

There are pheasants around still, and partridge, both the common and the red-legged, 'The Frenchman'. I was scouting for sweet-chestnut on the Bottom Park field one day when I saw a long line of red-legged partridge strung out as they walked over the crest of the hill just like the beaters who once would have driven them towards the guns.

Up in the woods is an old drinking fountain for gamebirds, a relic of the days when, as W. H. Hudson saw it of another place, 'the curse of the pheasant is on . . . all the woods and forests in Wiltshire'. Too many pheasants mean too many gamekeepers, wired-off coverts, watching eyes at dawn and dusk. No chance for the poacher or the clandestine farmer.

Lockleys Farm was pasture to the horizon for the first year I knew it. With nostalgia I recollect a bull called Harold and his herd of cows which kept the cowslip pasture grazed low, though its slope is too precipitous for any tractor. In the summer-time they and their calves wore paths down the slope as they came to drink at the trough in the valley. In the autumn there were rough shoots across the fields and the pigs were turned out to forage before a surfeit of acorns could harm the cows. As the winter brought snow, so the farmhands left long trails of hay to feed the cattle, or from a trailer pitchforked mangolds which skipped like ricocheting cannon balls down the hill-side. When the trough froze solid they would light straw fires underneath it to free the ballcock and melt the ice over the water.

And then the pasture disappeared. At first a methane pipe-line was brought down this dry spur valley of the Mimram. No sooner had that scar been reseeded and the pasture restored than George Baron sold the whole of the Bottom Park as turf. When the turfers had rolled the last sod away, the plough came in and has tilled it till now.

King Grain rules. These are barley lands. So much was needed to brew London's ale, that the oasthouses lining the river at Ware once formed the biggest malting complex in all Europe. Hertfordshire grew fat on beer by growing barley. But George Baron wasn't always a prairie farmer. He used to run a mixed economy: cows, pigs, barley and brussels sprouts. You could smell the sprouts half a mile away when the wind freshened up.

Now the pigs are kept close up to the farm together with the store cattle he buys in for fattening on the wet clay top pastures. Over the thirsty arable chalkland it is wheat, barley, oats. Then barley, wheat, barley. Then wheat and barley. But every year it's always barley.

Waving fields of corn isolate the old game coverts, which once had another function too, the coppiced woodland yielding hornbeam poles, a crop with a twelve-year cycle. Now that market has disappeared and the woods are returning to climax vegetation, untended, unused; but not unloved.

From the south side of this great bowl of Lockleys Farm, the side where I live, there are four woods to be seen. One, Lockleys, sends a probing line of trees down towards me, a beckoning finger which once was a windbreak to the glebelands where now there are houses, and remains as a shelter belt and squirrel route whose tip swells out to fill my garden with trees. Half a mile off, distance foreshortens the fields that lie between Foxley Grove, Whores Wood and Harmer Green Woods, while to the north and out of sight from here are two more wooded enclosures, Hazel Grove and Puttockhill Wood, and all of them leased to the Forestry Commission.

I had scoured these woods for food plants. Now I wondered what more could I make of all this? What anarchic rights could I exercise here without stealing, without disturbing ecological balance, without causing damage or depriving my fellow commoners of anything they valued? Rights of estovers, of turbary or pannage? I found scant relevance in ancient rights, as I did not seek to subsist on this land (though I might do well on hare, deer and barley-plump pigeon). But why should the rights claimed by medieval commoners be relevant today? They deal with fishing – but not in the manorial stewponds, the medieval equivalent of today's trout stream where fish are bred as a sportsman's crop; with taking turf for peat fires, gorse to charge the bakehouse oven, bracken for cattle bedding, pannage for pigs, of little use to the common man today. The taking of chalk was a 'right' I exercised, humping sacks of it from the field edge where it outcropped from Lockleys Wood, pulverizing it with a sledgehammer and dressing the ground of my vegetable patch in readiness for brassica seedlings. Mineral rights have normally rested with the lord of the manor as owner of the soil, and exploitation has usually meant mining. However, commoners at Aldbury in Hertfordshire are at liberty to take chalk from a common pit, and in theory the Common of

Marl still applies in parts of the New Forest. Marl is a mixture of chalk and clay which was used by farmers as a soil improver right up to the age of the bagged chemical fertilizer and is still considered by the Ministry of Agriculture to be 'very valuable' when applied to acid soils.

The marl pits on Lockleys Farm are overgrown with hornbeam, derelict dells. My soil might have responded to marling, but I decided to restrict my assumed 'right of common in soil' to collecting surface minerals.

Right of common has been described as the right to take some part of what another's land naturally contains or produces. The assumption of the Royal Commission on Common Land (1955–8) seemed to be that public access to common land today should be solely for 'air and exercise' although even here a court has ruled that *ius spatiandi* (a right to wander) cannot be the subject of claims based on ancient custom. Yet you will have read in my previous chapter that there are no restrictions on picking the common wild vegetables and fruits of the countryside. The admirable Conservation of Wild Creatures and Plants Act of 1975 restrains us only from picking the rarer flowers, and from uprooting plants. So, in the absence of prohibitions, there exists today by inference a right of forage enabling those who practise it to share a cultural link with their pastoral ancestors. This is the right I enjoyed to the full, and extended to the limit – the point where it becomes agriculture.

The appeal of the past is very clear to me, and if we fail to respond to it we stand to lose a great deal of our heritage. Fortunately the heritage I discover through the soil is reborn each year. If I fail to connect this year, if I miss the link between my life and lives gone by, the green book of nature will open its leaves to me again next spring, and for all my springs – and yours too.

# 5 Good King Henry

The land was becoming more familiar to me, I was identifying plants which could be of value. The next step was to organize my own activities to reap the maximum harvest. It is possible to distinguish stages of development in the practice of clandestine farming which all stem from the simple recognition of a wild plant or fruit which is good to eat. This is so frequently the blackberry that it is reasonable to call the first stage by the name of that plant, though there's a case for categorizing an even earlier stage, the moment when the child first accepts that a wild plant can be plucked and put in the mouth. The mother who sees her child chewing on a blade of grass, and tells him to throw it away, may be taking the first step in denying him a real understanding of his links with the earth. As a child, I heard wild stories about the leafhopper or aphid swallowed with the juice from a good green grass stem which would grow into an awful parasite in my stomach, and I laughed. But I remember the tales quite vividly and I am glad I didn't hear them from my parents.

Chewing grass apart, the phantom farmer will usually progress in this fashion:

1 Casual blackberrying, alone or in a group. An introduction to the wild harvest, though this fruit will be picked under each of the succeeding headings too.

2 Grazing. A delightful way to punctuate a country or seaside walk, varied in every season, chewing hawthorn buds in early spring, later a translucent beech leaf, a shoot of salad burnet from the meadow, with its lingering after-taste of cucumber; playfully doing the farmer's work, rolling an ear of corn and chewing the seeds, assessing the state of the harvest without any responsibility for gathering it; stooping by mudflats on an es-

tuary to break off stalks of the glasswort samphire and enjoying a refreshing salty finger salad. Your sense of taste will make the walk memorable.

3 Gathering. Now the harvest is deliberate, triggered by a seasonal event: the gleaning of corn from a field, an impromptu lifting of a crop of mushrooms which have appeared overnight in a meadow.

4 Foraging. A development of the earlier stages into a habit, once you have been alerted to the diverse resources of the earth, and are anxious to employ them economically. When undertaken communally, the nature of the task becomes competitive, if only at a game level, and there is a pleasure in comparing one's success with others even when the produce is to be pooled. The foraging instinct lies close to the surface, and you will fume with frustration when circumstances forbid the gathering of a giant puffball from a field or a useful piece of driftwood lumber from a beach. When armies 'liberate' the produce of an alien land they rapidly develop these habits. Not for nothing was the headgear of an off-duty soldier called a 'forage cap'.

5 Cropping – and an element of early agriculture creeps in. It may simply be the protection of a vulnerable crop from pests or human marauders. The work begins of tilling the soil, retarding competitive growth, cutting away shade plants, feeding the crop, transplanting a rootstock or sowing a seed. My first unconventional crop consisted of dandelions on my own lawn. I mowed around them, composted the plants, blanched leaves for salads and ultimately transplanted them to a corner of the vegetable garden for the roots to develop in friable soil and give me a good yield for roasting into 'coffee'.

6 Husbandry, which may be formal horticulture or farming, but when the land is not owned by the farmer is clandestine or phantom farming, of a natural crop, or sometimes a developed one – though the latter will be restricted to root crops in sandy soil, or ground-cover plants. Anything erect is usually too conspicuous.

That any of this progression can be a calculated method of acquiring food will seem preposterous to a person with a formal mind, or one tied to a conception of civilization as a progression of technical, social or scientific advances. Tell such a person that the countryside is your garden and they might well quote the White Queen in *Alice Through the Looking Glass*, saying, 'I've seen gardens compared to which this would be called a wilderness.'

To see the advantages of a garden in a wilderness calls for a special attitude of mind. For most of us, the country wilderness has a whole quality, but anyone who has picked a posy of flowers on a country walk has been conscious of the merit of the separate parts of the scene. When you can dissociate resources from their setting the notion of using them has already been conceived.

Many gardeners must have brought home wild flowers from the countryside to see if a protected habitat will encourage them to respond with new vigour and increased beauty. From the aesthetic notion it is easy to see the economic benefit you can derive from tending edible weeds with the same care you bestow on domesticated vegetables.

The first time I encountered the concept of clandestine farming was in a radical publication called *Food – Survival Scrapbook*. Here was outlined a plan for producing a proportion of one's food without needing to own the land on which it was grown. Plantings were to be of wild species such as dandelion and Good King Henry, or of inconspicuous cultivated crops such as root vegetables. By broadcasting seed, or planting in curved rows, the work of the gardener would less easily be discerned. It was suggested that the local pond might be stocked with fish for consumption when they reached maturity.

Although I suspected that this programme was not based on practical experience, and was more an inspired piece of dialectic, my own researches showed much of it to be feasible under favourable circumstances. There's a pond on Lockleys Farm too, but at the time I was farming, it was regularly fished by a heron and a kingfisher, so I decided to leave it to the professionals. A few years later, when the scrub which sheltered the birds had been cleared, my son and a friend discreetly introduced three large carp . . . meanwhile, I planned my planting.

Agriculture was born as soon as early man built some kind of seasonal or permanent camp. When you bring home nature's harvest it is probable you will shed the seeds of a new crop, by accident if not by design, and some will fall on your own threshold and by the paths you have worn. It takes little intelligence then to recognize the advantage of having your staple foods growing to hand, and – if you have seen seeds germinate – to try planting them yourself.

My first plan was to take regular walks across Lockleys Farm and into the surrounding woods, foraging for such useful resources as I could find. But the example of agriculture as a developed science lay all around me and there was no need for me to discover it afresh. Clearly, a grouping of plants of a like species would make it easier for me to gather them, and I could wage the war against competing plants on a narrower front.

Within a month of my initial exploration I was referring in my notebook to 'my' piece of Foxley Grove, a clearing some twenty feet by forty feet, three rods or so, which seemed best sited for my purpose. It was on a hillside facing south-east, well screened all round by trees yet close to the footpath. There were no defined paths anywhere in the wood, but in some places there were clear routes which a man would naturally follow, and none of these overlooked the clearing. On 29 April I had written: 'In my own open corner of Foxley Grove, bracken is dead and among it the bluebells are in flower and flourishing. There is dock, ground ivy, nettle, wild arum and some yellow archangel.'

It looked good then. But within a month I was describing the sensation of 'crunching through a salad of bluebell leaves, faded blue heads hanging low, outstripped by spikes of bracken. My vegetable plot? Little hope'.

As the bluebells died off, the bracken emerged rapidly, so that spikes between four and six inches high had grown before the bluebells died back. I knew the way the clearing would look before the summer was over if the bracken were not cut: an uninterrupted brake of fronds suppressing all but the most shade-loving herbage below.

Looking back, I have no clear recollection of what was in my mind all that summer as I kept the bracken under control. My diary shows that it was no heavy chore; but that I had my doubts of the outcome is clearly shown by those two words, 'little hope'. Yet I planned to establish one useful vegetable here and in time drive out the bracken – and I must have had *some* confidence in the plan. Success, however, depended in large measure on the vigorous growth and spread of the chosen vegetable. For my first crop I had selected *Chenopodium bonus Henricus*, Mercury Goosefoot or Good King Henry. I thought it could scarcely be bettered for the job ahead of me. Although considered a weed, it had formerly been cultivated in Europe and North America. In Germany it was *Guter Heinrich* and the Dutch name also translated to Good Henry in the sense of a good fellow, confirming the reputation summarized in an old saying:

> Be thou sick or whole
> Put mercury in thy koole [cabbage pot].

Good King Henry. It was going to be for me a potential greenstuff staple, every bit as good as spinach, and bulky enough to overcome the objection to most weeds as food, that they are too small. I studied pictures of Good King Henry, but failed to find it growing. As a naturalized plant I hoped to discover it near ancient habitations, a useful indicator that a kitchen garden had once existed there, the denizen surviving long after nature had reclaimed the land. The Hertfordshire *Flora* recorded its presence as 'occasional and well distributed in the county', on waste ground usually near to houses, but the plant distribution map of the species showed no records near Welwyn.

Finding seed was no problem. Several seed merchants who specialize in herbs list Good King Henry. I went to John Jefferies of Cirencester first, having read in their booklet on culinary herbs that it is 'easy to grow in almost any situation'. They described it as a hardy annual, and I accepted this description for a full year, until a new season brought an awakening to the dormant plant and to my consciousness of a writer's slip. All my earlier planning was based on an open cultivation of the plant with good spacing to give the annual seeds room to germinate. Had I known then it was a perennial I would have laid out many more seedlings the first year, instead of relying on a natural process of colonization.

There was one problem I had to contend with, a matter of conscience. An appreciation of ecology made me as reluctant to introduce a plant within a settled habitat as I would be to eliminate one from it. I could accept that my activities were going to displace some plants, but the most notable of these were bluebells and bracken. Bluebells already existed in the wood in their millions, unseen by all but the occasional trespasser, while curtailing the growth of the bracken would help other wild plants survive. The Botanical Society of the British Isles has produced a code of conduct for the conservation of wild plants which states unequivocally, 'Plants should not be introduced into the countryside without the knowledge and agreement of your local nature conservation Trust or natural history society.' Some clandestine farm this would be if each crop were subjected to open debate! As I saw it, the question was whether the plant existed in the countryside already. I went back to the distribution map, and the description 'well distributed', and decided that it did. I ordered the seeds with a clear conscience, and planted them in peat pots under glass.

On 10 June I set off for Foxley Grove with a sheath knife in my haversack. The young barley on the first field stood barely fifteen inches high, but the next field of wheat was in ear and between two and three feet tall. In the open by the edge of Foxley Grove the bracken stood erect still from last year, and in one place white bryony was ascending the dead fronds. I watched a pair of bullfinches by the edge of Lockleys Wood, where the chemical spray 'burn' was still in evidence. A yellowhammer flew up from the wheatfield as I climbed the fence into Foxley Grove.

At the corner where the footpath ends there are mounds of flints, probably dumped there clear of the field but looking also like the whitened bones of a tumbled cottage. There was a tiny clearing here, visible now from the footpath, but I knew that before long the bracken would screen it completely. The aspect was good, and I had decided to plant this clearing too. I could observe its progress without leaving the path, and would only need to stray a few yards to harvest the crop. With the knife, I cut down some nettles and all the bracken shoots in sight. The knife balanced well in my hand and the shoots were satisfyingly soft and glutinous for effortless execution. I moved deeper into the wood. When I reached the big clearing I thought at first I would chop the undergrowth unevenly, leaving random areas of uncut bracken as camouflage, but my enthusiasm carried me onwards and I worked right across a rectangle measuring twenty feet one way and thirty feet the other. I was in the middle of this task when I heard voices and felt both vulnerable and guilty.

It was almost impossible to guess the range, for on either side of the dry valley of the farm, sound is amplified by the natural bowl of the land. So pronounced was the effect that people speaking on the footpath less than fifty yards away sounded no nearer than others by the stile in Lockleys Wood, half a mile off. On this occasion I was relieved to see in the far distance a couple emerging from the woods over the railway tunnels, for I could easily be observed from the nearer path, and would need to be circumspect for a good few weeks to come, until the growing bracken hid my plot from view.

I walked home well pleased with my labour, observed in my passing only by two reed buntings who called out teasingly, 'see you-you, see you-you'.

The wild plants on the formerly grazed slope of the Bottom Park field continued to yield good green resources. There was sorrel in evidence, an astringent salad plant, but a good perennial greenstuff; there was mint; and I took home woodruff which smells like hay when dried, and was used in that state for putting with clothes as they aired, and as an addition to summer cups when green.

It was three weeks before I returned. In the cold frame the seeds of Good King Henry had germinated in peat pots, the first true leaves already displaying the triangular characteristic which gives them the family name goosefoot. Heavy rain had flattened three-quarters of the farmer's wheat crop but had brought on the colours of summer on the farm, the full range of green hues in the woods and hedgerows. The meadow slope was poised precariously at the pinnacle of display. The dog rose – which, with hawthorn, was bringing in a new dimension of growth – was in full flower over a square which measured twenty-five feet each way. In the past years cattle had given the shrubs no chance to take hold. They were on the ascendant now. But we could still enjoy the blossom-rich appearance of the former pasture, and today the scented orchid was giving a massed display. In one small area I counted fifty plants as I carried two gallons of water to the farm.

The ground certainly needed no water, but my aim was to build up a supply in gallon containers, never going empty-handed, and then to use the water during droughts. As I edged along the wheat field with my arms at full extension the back of one hand was kept at the level of the bramble shoots where they hung over the bank, and my wrist grew sore from scratches. But the bank revealed a compensating surprise: half a dozen wild strawberry plants, each plant yielding two or three tiny succulent strawberries, sweet and full flavoured.

I followed what looked like tractor tracks along the line of the ploughed-up footpath and stopped and stared when I reached the edge of Foxley Grove. The bracken by the fence stood some eight feet tall! I climbed over the fence with difficulty and dropped my water bottles on the other side. Even to reach the small cleared patch just inside the fence was an effort, so far advanced was the bracken growth. But it was principally at the edge of the wood, and under the trees nothing like such a dramatic advance was apparent. The cut patch was still clear. I slashed down a few new bracken shoots with my knife, and piled those which were in leaf with some goosegrass I pulled up, to form an embryo compost heap.

It was a warm, fine evening, and before long I was sweating, and plagued by flies. I used the knife to hack holes in the stony, sandy soil ready to receive the first plants. Around each hole I arranged a circle of flints with a dual purpose: to collect dew and thus water the soil, and to deflect sunlight so that evaporation was slowed down.

As I finished the job I noticed a foxglove flowering among the massed bracken, and thought that if it could survive against such odds, why should not Good King Henry flourish too? In the main clearing there were fresh bracken shoots to trim back, and I worked until eight o'clock. As I was walking home, the smell of decomposing stinkhorn hung on the still air, but as usual I failed to narrow down the search sufficiently for my eyes to take over identification from my nose!

We had a week of sunshine then, and after a Saturday spent sunbathing I thought the time had come to move the first few plants from the relative shelter of the garden to the farm. In the weeks ahead they would receive scant attention, but I was determined that they would start their lives with every advantage. Accordingly I arranged them carefully in my haversack and gathered two bags of mulch. One I carried in my hand, a paper sack stuffed with wood chippings. On my back was a frame rucksack, and inside it a plastic sack containing compost. I reasoned that my unsterilized compost would succour the plants but also introduce new seedling rivals, so if the compost were overlaid with a woodchip mulch this would serve to stifle the alien seed growth at birth . . .

Again it was fine as I set off at 5.30 in the afternoon, feeling very conspicuous. I am certainly happier when my portage coincides with a downpour which keeps other people indoors, and I often wonder what I will say to the farmer if I meet him so encumbered that comment of some kind is inevitable. What answer is there to the question 'What have you got there?' when it is a gallon of water, or a scythe with the head unscrewed to be carried less conspicuously in my pocket? What friendly answer can be anything but evasive, or mad, or even implausibly true? I have from time to time invented relevant deceits to conceal the facts, but have never been called upon to voice them. I doubt if I have been suspected of anything other than poaching, and that only on those occasions when a bulging haversack has been the subject of scrutiny.

I had reached the corner of Foxley Grove before I had a scare. In the distance a red anorak. It didn't look like a farmworker – it was probably a rambler – but I quickly scaled the fence and made straight for the main clearing by a circular route, so I wouldn't be visible from the footpath. I intended skirting the patch and entering from the side so as to leave the full growth of bracken undisturbed as a screen both above and below my plot. But I misjudged and had made a track through the bracken and emerged into the open before I expected to, so spoiling my cover for a future occasion.

It was a satisfying moment, however, climaxing months of planning, conjecture, philosophizing. I settled four plants into the shallow soil, fingers conscious of the ever-present rhizomes of bracken as I worked the surface mould into a paste to keep the peat pots soft and encourage the emergence of roots. A fifth plant was similarly introduced to the smaller clearing by the path, and I murmured a prayer for new growth, and watered them all in.

A week later I was back, in the wake of a cloudburst that initially justified my wearing full waterproof rig. Later, it grew hot, and with an Amazonian mist hanging over the valley, I was to suffer. I took two more gallons of water with me to increase the irrigation stocks, and a puffer of pyrethrum. The upper plot was in good shape. I pulled some rival greenery from around my young plants and started a new compost heap. Over the hill the Sunday chimes which marked six o'clock from Welwyn Church tower reminded me of a conventional thanksgiving. Alone on the hillside this transgressor felt elated, quite unrepentant, and gave thanks in his heart, in his own way . . .

On the lower plot the solitary plant had a pale green mealy infestation which was deforming its leaves. I puffed it with pyrethrum, and planted a companion in another stone-mulched hollow before setting off for a walk the long way home. I put up two partridge and watched coaltits before I reached Harmer Green Woods. Under the pine trees I found toadstools, just one species: the Blusher – not good eating.

Later that month I was away in Yorkshire with the family, researching mills and mill lore, whortling on Brimham Heights and enjoying the juicy berries the way I prefer all soft fruit – transferred straight from plant to lips.

On our return the harvest was under way. One field of barley had already been cleared when I took a Sunday evening walk in the rain to Foxley Grove, walking through the unharvested field along Footpath 30, whipped by the heavy wet heads of wheat. The barley which had not yet been combined was golden still, but the wheat, as I looked over the whole sweep of the field, was going black from days of rain. Fine weather for Good King Henry, bad weather for old George Baron. The screening bracken along the fence had collapsed under its damp top weight, and on the ground one of my two plants had died down, but a tiny new shoot had emerged. I cut down new bracken shoots and went to the top clearing, where all was well.

I left my farm to look after itself – which was part of the policy, as my selected crop was intended to be a natural survivor – and returned late in August. Where the combines had taken the wheat crop you could see that the field bindweed – so much in evidence last month on the outside stalks – had flourished over the entire field, evidence supporting the herbicide makers who admit they cannot eliminate weeds, only control them. Along the edge of Lockleys Wood were the best blackberries to be found on the farm. I browsed my way along the bramble bushes to Footpath 38. A farmworker on a tractor was pulling a side rake along the barley straw by the edge of Foxley Grove, apparently clearing it from the perimeter prior to firing. One field was already burned, and I walked across the striped earth, compacted strips in the pattern of combine tracks alternating with bands of smelly black stubble.

In my own garden the cosseted plants of Good King Henry were making impressive progress, and on 30 August I collected black seeds from the ripened heads of the best specimen. I had resolved not to pick the leaves of any of the plants on the farm, although I did wonder if regular stripping of the outer leaves might actually encourage growth. I decided that fresh growth was to be stimulated when I was using the plants as food, but that right now I wanted each plant to use all its vigour to produce and distribute an abundance of seed.

On 23 September I stripped all the Good King Henry plants in the garden of their leaves and steamed them for five minutes in a saucepan containing just a little boiling salted water. We all had some with our lunch. It was like spinach, which we like, though my wife found it rather stronger. I thought it was very tasty then, and I still do.

All through the year, my foraging expeditions across the farm had been carried out between hours spent working on my conventional kitchen garden at home, and all the time I was making comparisons between these two quite different ways of finding sustenance. Superficially the difference was between a respectable enterprise and an exercise which, however meticulously I attempted to keep within the law, would seem secretive, and probably reprehensible, to most of my neighbours. I was conscious of deeper differences. My gardening was labour-intensive. When my motor mower broke down I got rid of it and went back to the old hand mower to take a compost crop off the lawn. I put aside thoughts of rotavators, and dug new ground – to remove some of the glacial drift in pebble form called soil hereabouts and some of the still live tree roots – until my back ached. As I dug, or sifted stones, or planted rows of seedlings, even though the scale of the operation was small, the single-minded repetition of the job stultified thought, and left my mind an intellectual vacuum into which was drawn the coda of a current song or the constant reiteration of a pointless phrase. Knowing that I could never remove all the stones – and not wishing to – I justified the removal of those that came to hand with the thought: I am removing a significant proportion of the stones. Curiously, and eventually maddeningly, this sterile phrase came to mind every time I picked stones and was turned over and over as though my by now apparently automated intellect would find a greater significance from the words through familiarity. It never did.

In contrast, any activity connected with the clandestine farm was enlightening, entertaining, and stimulated my brain to the extent that a visit undertaken without pencil and notebook was bound to bring frustration as I struggled to memorize phrases, concepts, incidents until the time I could commit all to paper. Ideas came brimming to the surface like bubbles of oxygen from pond plants, a wholly beneficial response to my environment which enabled me to survive even the disappointment of my first lost crops.

# 6 Hunter's moon

There are three main reasons for hunting animals: for the pleasure of the chase; for the value of the carcass; or to eliminate the quarry as vermin or a potential aggressor. I take no pleasure in killing, but find the logic of the remaining arguments in favour of hunting is inescapable.

On my smallholding I was in competition not only with the established plant life, but with animals too. For a while I abandoned my strict attitude towards plant introductions and attempted to raise haricot and soya beans on the unlikely soil, defiantly acid and gravel. At first I would be encouraged by their response to my careful watering, but inevitably there came the day when the only evidence that plants had been in that spot was a row of close-cropped stalks.

Nor did the predators stop short at domesticated plants. Having trowelled all the dandelions out of my lawn to make dandelion coffee I decided to transform one clearing into a coffee plantation. From a score of 'clocks' I raised dandelion seedlings and transplanted them haphazardly to naturalize in the clearing, but before ever they could establish themselves they were eaten.

Netting would have given away my activities, so I tried heaping branches and spiky dead hawthorn twigs around the seedlings to deter marauders – rabbits I imagined, although their droppings were sparse – but nothing survived. In the end another hunter, a fox, did what I should have done for myself and left severed limbs and tufts of rabbit fur amongst the grass of the clearing. I found more evidence of indiscriminate slaughter by foxes on another good growing site I had cleared – the carcass of a young heron was lying almost untouched as food – and I prepared to plant out some vulnerable crops as soon as rain had fallen; hoping the rabbits might have been frightened off.

So much of what the naturalist wants to see in the countryside happens at night-time. He has to be content with detective work, looking for tracks, analysing the pellets of birds of prey and the fumets of deer to discover who is eating what! It is almost akin to archaeology, but the inhabitants whose lives you reconstruct are alive and the patient watcher can see them if he waits by moonlight.

For humans, the formal business of hunting is delayed until the harvest is in, otherwise the cost of making restitution for trampled crops sours the sport of killing the fox. After the harvest moon comes the hunter's moon, and at eight o'clock on 6 September it turned the flat slope of burned stubble fields into a floodlit stage. I was following the perimeter of Foxley Grove, now impenetrably black. It wasn't a normal route for me, being in full view of the farm in daylight and a good hundred yards from the public footpath. The field was fenced, but near the wood's edge was a gate and I made for it from my side just as a fox trotted towards it from the other side. We reached the gate and saw each other at the same moment, and he turned his bushy tail on me and silently disappeared down the hill. I climbed the fence, walked after him a little way, then moved into the shadow of the trees and lay down in the grass to see if he would return.

The advice of a gamekeeper named Monty Penny came to mind: 'Two hours at daybreak and two at dusk are worth eight hours any other time. Vermin always hunt food at dusk, then again at dawn.' So the fox was off on the hunt. Surely he would not abandon it simply through a chance encounter with a human? If I was identified as a passing threat he might simply lie low until I had moved away. I lay with my ear in the dark world of insect life, motionless, trying to reason a fox's conduct, an anthropomorphist at large. Fifteen minutes passed and then the fox returned, trotting up the field with all the assurance he had shown as he approached the gate initially, his ears pricked forward as he came closer and closer, silhouetted in the bright moonlight. He was twenty feet from me when he suddenly turned and raced down the hill, pausing only once, and then briefly, at the far limit of my vision.

This fox was not yet hunting; he was foraging just as the fox was who came on five golden pheasants we had reared in our garden and butchered them all on their roost. I have sat in the ditch of a fire-break in nearby Bramfield Forest awaiting a spring dawn when the woodcock was roding, and heard the sharp terrier-like bark of a fox in the wood on one side answered by another on my side of the ride. *They* were hunting, using teamwork to startle game from the sound of one into the jaws of the other.

Now the fox had helped me by killing my competitor. But I could have enjoyed eating rabbit if I had done the killing; why was I reluctant to compete with the fox?

Most hunters I meet are 'sportsmen'. The pigeons they shoot are left to rot – or are exported. Anglers carry a device for humanely removing the barbed hook from the fish's mouth before they return the fish to the water. Gamebirds are bred for the gun and guided by beaters right to the barrel, which is hardly hunting.

Like many others, I was taught from the age of sixteen in 'peacetime' to use rifle, machine-gun, bayonet and mortar. My children are entertained from books and from television with dramas in which men kill men. We show our offspring how to kill their own kind, while shielding them from experience of killing to eat.

The only time I have been to the cinema and seen people leave because they could not stand the images on screen was at a showing of Georges Franju's *Le Sang des Bêtes.* It is a documentary, filmed with compassion in the abattoirs of Paris, in 1949. There is no false melodrama, no villain. We stand close by while men skilfully convert frightened animals into meat. The pace at which the work is carried out is such that from the initial shock – the moment of stunned spasm – until the carcass is stacked, drained and gutted, there is no respite for the eye. Blood gushes in torrents. The animals are so big: guts tumble like a living, obscene avalanche. The slaughter house steams, reeking of death and gore. Anyone who eats meat without knowing that this task is performed daily on his behalf, who fails to understand or deliberately dismisses that knowledge, is a hypocrite. And yet this sight is more secret than the hospital, the cemetery, the asylum, and Franju's film was shown in England during a National Film Theatre season titled 'The Anarchist Cinema'.

While I eat meat, I am prepared to kill my prey, skin or pluck it and draw it. And when I cannot bear the act of killing I will cease to eat meat. I think that may be soon.

There is no need for us to eat meat, and to use grazing animals as protein converters is a land-wasting form of husbandry. Better to grow beans – as Thoreau did. In time we may be forced to become vegetarians, all of us, and our hunting instincts – part of our inherited aggression – may disappear. But while we compete with other animals for the same food plants, the best economic use we can make of those animals is to eat them. If you call me cruel, 'no better than a beast', when I talk of shooting a pigeon or snaring rabbit, the first thing I will ask you is, do you eat meat?

There is no closed season for shooting wood-pigeon, and it is a lawful act providing you are the owner or authorized occupier of the land on which the shooting is done. It has no effect on the wood-pigeon population, which reaches a peak in Britain of some ten million birds in September after breeding, and has dropped to about five million by July largely through starvation during the winter months. R. K. Murton says that 'shooting mortality is not additional to natural mortality and could only be so if the number killed by shooting exceeded the number that have to die in any case'.

Pigeons are at their plumpest between October and December, but gourmets prefer birds taken in the spring or early autumn when they are corn-fed and likely to have the best flavour. The task of providing this addition to our larder was initially given to my eldest son, Paul. Armed with a .22 air rifle and settled in a hide made from straw bales, he waited morning after morning for the dawn arrival of pigeons. They came; he fired, and missed. It doesn't matter too much where the slug hits the bird – it will go right through any part except the breastbone. But you should aim to hit the head, so you kill rather than cripple. His problem was, he was trying too hard. One day he loosed off a fairly casual shot, and down came the bird. From then on he remembered to squeeze, not snatch, the trigger and his tally of shot birds mounted.

The professional pigeon shooter uses a shotgun, but it is not necessary to incur the cost of cartridges (three per bird on average), provided you restrict yourself to shooting the sitting bird.

You will only be able to shoot on relatively windless days, and you will need an accurate rifle – preferably one which has lever reloading rather than a barrel which is hinged. The .22 pellet is twice as heavy as the .177 and twice as effective. It will kill at up to fifty yards. One big advantage of the air rifle is its quiet report, sometimes permitting a second shot at the prey you have missed first time!

When disturbed, wood-pigeons take flight back to tree cover, so we had continual visitors to our garden coppice. There was the water tank and pond in the Bottom Park field where the birds would drink, and there was the attraction of the farmer's corn crop as well as my own vegetables to bring them in. Paul also tried decoys, cunningly painted cardboard models first of all, stylized birds sporting the white wing and neck marks. These are part of the bird's signalling pattern and elicit a response from others of the species, particularly those which are hungry. They should be set out with the majority facing head to wind, at least a dozen of them. Next we made a decoy by injecting formaldehyde into the flesh of a shot bird (after cutting out the breast for the pot) and then stuffing and mounting it. Within minutes of our standing it on the lawn, a magpie alighted and attacked it with vigour!

A shot bird is quickly sought out by flies, and the carcass should preferably be kept somewhere cool and fly-free before it is plucked and drawn. Pigeon is best eaten fresh. I pluck the birds as soon as possible – a fiddly business, but wings (always the most difficult to pluck) can be cut off at the first joint. If the bird is young, fresh and in good condition it is worth preparing it whole, after removing head and feet, and taking the crop contents out through the slit neck and eviscerating through the slit stomach. You can serve them spit-grilled or roasted. If you have a glut you can just eat the pigeon breasts.

The crop content will show you who is keeping the pigeon: it's the farmer. The crops of the birds we shoot are normally stuffed with grain, with very little greenstuff to be seen. A neighbour of Gilbert White's shot a dove in 1788 and his wife served it up on a plate garnished with its own last supper – turnip tops which she had washed and boiled after removing them from the bird's crop! In exchange for an annual loss to the farmer at 1965 values of something like 50p worth of produce per bird on his land, we as a nation have at any one time 2000 tons of pigeon meat on the wing – and it's good food.

A pigeon makes a meal for one, a snack for two. I like them best casseroled with cider, as in this recipe from *A Pigeon for the Pot*:

*Ingredients*
4–6 pigeon breasts
2 bacon rashers
1 large onion
½ lb mushrooms
½ pt cider
¼ pt stock
bay leaf
seasoning
flour

*Method*
Place pigeon breasts on bacon rashers in a casserole. Cover with finely shredded onion, add bay leaf and pour over ½ pt of cider. Leave overnight and then cook, tightly covered, in a low oven for about two hours. Then add mushrooms, top with a little stock if necessary, and cook for another hour or so until the pigeons are quite tender. Before serving, remove bay leaf; thicken and season gravy to taste. (Serves 4)

One April morning I was walking up in Harmer Green Woods when I spied a small rabbit sitting on the top of a chalky hummock. Quietly I approached and stood right by it for two or three minutes. The breathing was irregular, the eyes closed, the eyelids reddened. It sat under a dog rose with white flowers around it, and a chiff-chaff, a blackbird and a chaffinch sang a requiem. I thought that death could not be far off, but when I moved it scampered off. It's you who own this land as much as any of us, I thought philosophically.

It took some time to adjust to the idea of eating rabbit. I had the snares long before I set them. Primarily the problem was that there were actually very few rabbits on the farm. I see a hare fairly frequently sitting out in the fields, or I startle it from its form in the woods and it leaps away. But the only place I expect to see the 'sloppeting' gait of departing rabbits is on pastures to the east of Harmer Green Woods – where there are cattle I'd be as likely to snare as I would the rabbits.

Then there's the question of myxomatosis. Rabbits nowadays can survive it, but the scar tissue on their faces is so obvious you need be in little doubt whether the animal has had the disease or not. I felt I would know a healthy rabbit. The disease is by no means endemic. With an apparent change of habit in some areas towards surface breeding, new generations of 'top rabbits' have emerged, less prone to infect each other with the myxomatosis-carrying flea.

Tender-heartedness comes into it too. Sitting in a hide one dawn in the New Forest, waiting for deer to emerge, I watched the close relationship between adult and young rabbits, playing in families. To snare one seemed so cruel. But the domestic idyll is short-lived for the young rabbit 'kittens', even though their parents may mate for life – which on average will be eighteen months. Unless the litter is the last of the season, the doe abandons them during the fourth week.

Similar guilt feelings concerning wood-pigeons were assuaged once I learnt that the young 'squeakers' are fed in the nest for only twenty-two days, and seven days after that they are left to fend for themselves as fledglings. No lifelong family bonds there, either.

The final problem was the law. To catch all the references to rabbits on the statute book you would need to put a net around the Game Laws like a ferreter at a warren. Under the Theft Act of 1968 it is not possible to *steal* a hare or rabbit from private land, because while running wild they have not been 'reduced into possession'. But curiously, if you pick up a dead rabbit from the road after you have run over it in your car, you may be guilty of theft.

The clandestine farmer who adds a little meat to his diet is more likely to be found guilty of poaching. After John and Sally Seymour had written *Self Sufficiency*, John was quoted as saying of his publishers, 'Faber asked me to cut out most of the references to poaching in my book.' It is clear enough that the average Briton views poaching as a minor infringement of the law, akin to smuggling an extra bottle of spirits through the Customs, a peccadillo referred to with a nudge and a wink amongst otherwise law-abiding citizens. Having bred pheasants myself, and knowing the cost of rearing broods, I would leave the true gamebirds – as I would the tank-bred trout – to their rightful owners. But an animal which is acknowledged by all parties as a pest is quite another matter. Nevertheless, there is the law to be considered, and if you go for rabbits, know your law – if only to be able to confound gamekeeper or constable on a technicality.

I respect all laws concerning firearms, however. I'd rather be a nuisance than a menace. That's why we use a .22 air rifle with great care in our garden and rarely elsewhere. Take rabbits with snares for preference, though inevitably there's controversy over their use. The British Field Sports Society say snares may involve a good deal of cruelty, but 'abolition . . . without an effective alternative, could lead to the use of more undesirable methods'. The Game Conservancy does not approve of snaring either, but says it is, at present, 'the only control method that is at all effective'.

Dismissing all snaring as potentially cruel, some people advocate cyanide, but this hardly helps the poacher who wants a free meal. Three types of snare have been used since the gin-trap was banned. The stop snare does not strangle the victim, but holds it firmly until dispatched by the hunter. The potential cruelty here is that another predator – a fox, say – may devour the captive before you do. The lock snare draws tighter and tighter, inflicting cruel wounds on an animal which may be caught by a leg rather than round the neck. The running noose throttles the animal unconscious, but then slackens, possibly allowing it to recover and struggle towards repeated strangulation. I state all this because when you use a trap you should appreciate the possible consequences and act responsibly as far as you can. This means never setting a snare unless you are sure you can check it early the next morning. Rabbits run at nightfall and daybreak.

Night is the poacher's friend, but the gamekeeper is most wary of the night poacher, not knowing whether he is just a local looking for a meal, or one of a gang with a freezer to fill and guns to help them fill it. Not surprisingly, the law frowns most on armed poachers, night poachers and gangs of poachers (particularly if there are five or more together).

The Night Poaching Act of 1828 proscribes the offence of unlawfully taking or destroying any game or rabbits by night on any land open or enclosed, or unlawfully entering or being upon such land at night with any gun, net, engine or other instrument for the purpose of taking or destroying game.

Night starts at the expiration of the first hour after sunset and ends at the beginning of the last hour before sunrise. The offence extends to any public road, highway or path or the sides thereof or at the openings, outlets or gates into any such road, highway or path.

Poaching by day is the subject of several statutes. Although there are many exceptions where rabbits are concerned, the Game Licence Act of 1860 covers the offence of taking, killing or pursuing game, woodcock, snipe, coney (rabbit) or deer without a game licence. The Game Act of 1831 refers to committing a trespass by entering or being in the daytime upon any land in search of or pursuit of game, woodcock, snipe, or conies. If apprehended, the trespasser may be required by the owner, occupier, gamekeeper or police constable to give his name and address and quit the land. If he refuses these requests he may be arrested. But it is essential for the trespasser to be *asked* to give his address. If that information is not requested, the arrest is not lawful.

Finally, there is the Poaching Prevention Act of 1862 which authorizes any constable or peace officer to stop and search any person or vehicle in any highway, street or public place, whom he may have good cause to suspect of coming from any land where he shall have been unlawfully in search of or pursuit of game. Game here includes rabbits and hares, and it is not necessary that the defendant should have succeeded in catching any. It is sufficient if it is shown that the gun, cartridge, net, trap or snare which may be produced as incriminating evidence has been used with the intention of unlawfully taking game.

We began within the law. My son was working with a friend on a neighbouring farm, and they were given permission to set snares for rabbits. They took to it like natural, born poachers. Actually, as James Bateman has pointed out, 'rabbits and hares are perhaps among the easiest animals to trap, despite their acutely sensitive hearing and keen sense of smell', and says that 'young boys generally count rabbits among their first trap victims, and hungry trappers out of luck with other animals have generally been able to fill their stewpot with the assistance of a wire noose set on a rabbit trail'.

Although the rabbit has apparently no instinctive awareness

of traps, skill is still required in setting snares. The victim will not go out of his way to put his head in the noose. It must be at the height of his head, on a regular run, and preferably at the point on the run where the animal is moving at its fastest. If you develop the backwoods skills sufficiently, or have the patience to study your prey alive before you seek to take it dead, you may be able to eliminate much of the chance of failure.

The poacher will cast his experienced eye over a rabbit run and note patches of flattened grass. He will deduce that his rabbit habitually leaps an obstacle – perhaps just a grass tuft – and lands at this point. Visualizing that leap, he sets his snare just past the obstacle, a pear-shaped noose, four fingers' width from the ground. But he judges the distance rather than measures it, so that the scent of his hand will not hang over the run. Where runs adjoin, the snare on one is set some distance from the snare on the other, so the struggles of one victim will not scare off a second before he, too, is trapped.

In *The Amateur Poacher* Richard Jefferies provides a meticulous description of his youthful attempts to make a snare, and how at length he perfected the design. Gilbertson and Page sell a range; I bought a dozen readymade, at a country hardware store. The 'wires' should be hung out of doors to weather for a week or two while you cut ash stoles of walking-stick thickness to make plugs or pegs which, when driven hard into the earth, will make the snare secure. Whittle a point on each plug and cut a groove all round its other end to take the cord of the snare. The noose is held clear of the ground by a thinner stick, the teeler. Cut pencil-thin shoots of hazel for the job. The stick is sharpened to penetrate the ground, and its upper tip is notched and split to hold the shank of the wire. The bark is left on the teelers, and together with the pegs they are buried in loose earth for a few days to weather and stain, and lose their human scent. When setting the snares with these tethering and setting pins, run your hands well in dry earth or grass, or wear gloves. The rabbit's nose may scare him off if his eyes do not.

I have watched the keeper on the Brocket Estate harl a rabbit with his knife the way Richard Jefferies describes it, 'passing the blade of the knife between the bone of the thigh and the great sinew – where there is nothing but skin – and then thrusting the other foot through the hole thus made', so that the catch can hang and the blood run to its head. John Seymour advises his readers to gut or 'hulk' rabbits as soon as they catch them, but not hares which are game and should hang. What Jefferies calls harling, Seymour calls 'hocking', and says a countryman does it without a knife, using the sharp claw of the rabbit's own foot! But if you want to eat your fill of rabbit you will carry your catch home by his ears, and drain the blood off later to keep for soup.

Paul's first efforts with a snare were rewarded with a fine rabbit, whether through beginner's luck, or skill, I don't know. Subsequently he found it to his advantage to convert them into cash by arrangement with our local family butcher, but not before we had enjoyed rabbit stew and rabbit pie.

Snares have been used since palaeolithic man's day, so it is not surprising that many refinements have been developed and have passed into backwoods lore. Some of these are concerned with protecting your catch from other hunters, once the snare has done its job. You may want to bleed your catch but prefer not to have a stoat do it for you. The stoat drains off the warm blood from a trapped rabbit, leaving the flesh chicken-white. The marauding magpie pecks out its eyes. But the fox takes all.

One way to defeat these other hunters is to tie a few tins to the tethering cord so the movements of the snared rabbit (if he lives) may warn off marauders. More sophisticated, and more effective too, is the hanging snare in which the trapper's wire is set as normal, but fastened to a sapling which is bent over and secured to the ground by a pair of notched wooden pins. Once disturbed, the pins disengage and the sapling springs up, twitching the catch with it, so that it hangs suspended out of harm's way.

If a rabbit survives the snare, dislocate its neck by giving a chopping blow with the edge of the hand behind the ears, while holding it up in the other hand by the legs. Alternatively, hold the hind legs in one hand while the other grips the rabbit round the neck, fingers under the chin and your thumb on top of its head (but take care that you don't get bitten). Now stretch the animal while turning back its head to dislocate the neck.

Slit the stomach with a knife and the guts are easily pulled out and discarded. Keep the heart and liver. Cut off the head and feet, and slit the fur centrally up the underside with the point of your knife just under the fur, leaving the skin uncut. Now you can tug the pelt back bit by bit, peeling it from the body whole, like a coat.

If you want to keep the skin, remove this before you gut the animal so as to keep the pelt as intact as possible. Hang the rabbit by one leg on a hook passed between bone and tendon, below the hock. Cut around the fur below each hock, remove the tail and slit up each back leg. Cut around the neck and forefeet, then pull the skin down and over the rabbit's head, tugging it off firmly. If the animal is freshly killed the skin comes away quite easily. Carefully separate any fat from the skin.

While the skin is still warm pull it on to a stretcher (straighten out a heavy wire coat-hanger and give it a turn around a broom handle to make a spring with two long prongs). Keep both forefeet on one side and hold the lower end of the skin closed with a clothes peg to prevent it curling, while it hangs to dry in an airy place. When the skin is dry, slit it down the belly and soak it for at least two hours in water which must be changed several times. Soak too long, however, and the fur may drop out. When it has softened, use a blunt knife to scrape the skin clean of flesh and fat. Dissolve 1 oz of washing soda in a gallon of water to give the skin a final wash, then squeeze it out. Soak a rag in petrol and go over the inside of the skin, removing any grease or dirt.

To tan the skin, dissolve 1 lb of salt in a gallon of water, using a glass or earthenware vessel. Taking great care not to splash yourself or inhale the fumes, stir in 1 oz of concentrated sulphuric acid. When the solution has cooled, immerse the skin and keep it covered for up to three days, giving it a stir from time to time. Then rinse it in cold water. Dissolve 1 oz of borax in a gallon of water and work the skin in this for ten minutes. Rinse again, squeeze the skin dry and work it in your hand for a while before pinning it, stretched flat, on a board. Dress the skin with a thin layer of butter, or neatsfoot oil from a saddler's, and leave it to dry. Finally, remove it from the board and work it backwards and forwards vigorously over the edge of a table, fur side up. If the inside of the skin still feels rough after this, it may be lightly sandpapered. Sandpapering, soaking and working the skin may be necessary at any time after it has been washed.

If you end up with a few skins, make a Davy Crockett hat from them. If you are feeling more ambitious, try a waistcoat!

I had hoped to use tannin from oak bark for my skin curing, but the old oak bark which I could strip from fallen timber contains little tannin. You should use the inner phloem of young bark – kept dry to avoid the tannin leaching out – cut up, ground and mixed with water. Hides were kept in the strong solution for two years to make shoe leather. I decided my coney skins would be unlikely to survive such harsh treatment without going bald! If you have hides you want to tan, read how to do it in *Woodland Crafts in Britain* by Herbert Edlin.

It has been said that snaring has little excitement, and certainly it smacks more of a ruse than a hunt. You can hunt your rabbit with a gun, shoot at him with bow and arrow or catapult, or try mesmerizing him by pursing your lips and sucking in air to make a high-pitched squeak – which, with luck, may make the rabbit sit up and gaze at you, hypnotized – and then hope your aim is good enough to bring him down with the rock you hurl.

For myself, I would prefer to be as calculating, as businesslike, as unemotional about the trapping process as I could be. Blood lust demeans me as a human being. Unlike the animal which has no decision to make, which is faced with no choices, we have our lives to fill and may choose how we fill them. I hope to find happiness through absorption in life-enhancing activities, rather than in those which deal death. But hunting has always been a favoured pastime, as the Spanish philosopher José Ortega Y Gasset reminds us, the chosen occupation of the privileged through the ages. Having claimed that hunting is for most men a form of bliss, he considers that man is an animal still, only on the road to becoming rational, by no means yet a rational being, that his history includes carnivorous origins as well as those of a herbivore, so that 'man in fact combines the two extreme conditions of the mammal, and therefore he goes through life vacillating between being a sheep and being a tiger'. Because the past is always viewed with the knowledge of hindsight, and the dilemmas of earlier ages are now mellowed by the knowledge of how men coped with them, we nostalgically look back in search of a longed-for Golden Age. But all historical ages were the outcome of the influences that applied in that time, rather than now, so no return to them can be anything but charade. Only a simulated return to prehistory permits man to take a holiday from the human condition, and only the wild animal in a wild landscape calls man to a prehistoric existence, to be again a hunter.

Thus the principle which inspires hunting for sport is that of artificially perpetuating, as a possibility for man, a situation which is archaic in the highest degree: that early state in which, already human, he still lived within the orbit of animal existence.

I have maintained that in all the historical possibilities explored by man to alleviate the human condition, somewhere there might be one or many that could apply to us, today. Ortega denies this. 'Man is condemned to an inability to be substantively happy if he cannot be happy in the style of his own time.'

So the only escape for him is to relive a timeless situation – one embodying the relationship which has always existed between hunter and hunted – but to relive it in the style of our own time. Ortega accepts game reserves and game laws which protect the animals, and hunting rifles which are the present-day weapon of the hunter, but maintains that once the hunt begins the gap between the hunter and palaeolithic man diminishes. The animal defines the hunter. For the animal, fear is permanent, it is its way of life, its occupation, and the only adequate response to a being that lives obsessed with avoiding capture is to try to catch it.

If we are to benefit from this release, this primitive return – the argument goes on – we must preserve the spirit of the hunter, which is aggression. Our need to kill may not be so intense as once it was, nevertheless the wish to kill is necessary. We must emulate the animal in the subtle rite called hunting.

Another writer has suggested that the hunters of our past were more fully human than their descendants who invented agriculture and condemned man to a toil that was rarely a vocation – as hunting might be. For Paul Shepard, a return to nature by no means implies 'backtracking through the barnyard'. Only through a regression to the hunter-gatherer kind of society can we blossom to full freedom. The farm epitomizes drudgery and a jealous attitude to property, and he quotes Marshall Sahlins: 'A few people are happy to consider few things their good fortune. It is consistent with their mobility that among hunters needs are limited, avarice inhibited, and portability is a main value in the economic scheme of things.'

But before we can attain this happy attitude of self-sufficiency we must readjust to the animal prey which provides the key to it. 'First man must unlearn his misconception of the animal as a brute.' It is not inconsistent, says Shepard, both to extol the animal, to worship it even, and then to kill it, providing the killing is done with respect, and is justified by subsequent consumption of the corpse.

> All animals are predatory (or parasitic) since they obtain and eat other organisms. Carnivores, which eat meat, must catch, kill and dismember their prey. Man is in part a carnivore; the male of the species is genetically programmed to pursue, attack and kill for food. To the extent that men do not do so they are not fully human.

Children should be encouraged in the study of anatomy ('those who cannot stand the sight of intestines, blood, or death have been cruelly removed from reality') but the carcass must not be wasted. Only when the sacred act of eating the prey is neglected does the killing become shameful: 'Assimilation is a suitable expression of love.'

I immersed myself in these arguments while seeking also every sentiment which tended to refute them. I could, and did, adopt either stand both resolutely and indiscriminately in formal debate and private conversation. But I found it more and more a hypothetical question in view of the conflicting demands of nature conservation and population growth. There was little enough room or resources for domesticated meat, let alone for wild game.

# 7 Autumn

Autumn is traditionally a time to be like the squirrel, to hoard food against the onset of winter while the plants are making provision for a resting season and a rebirth.

The ripening hedgerow declares the arrival of blackberry time, and all over the country people who have never plucked so much as a leaf from the ground to add to a salad, sally out armed with bowls, saucepans, cardboard boxes and baskets to reap the harvest. Some fruit will be eaten straight from the bush, some will be picked over, graded and examined for maggots before receiving a libation of cream on each fresh portion. The rest will be bottled as jam, puréed, or frozen to provide a taste-and-colour contrast to apple pies through the winter. Blackberry remains the great traditional countryside harvest, the one free crop that is not wholly neglected.

I remember an afternoon idling by narrow boat along the Grand Union Canal, beguiled by laden blackberry bushes along the banks trailing their fruit to water level. It would be worth the effort to launch a good broadbeamed dinghy there. I spent a day on Offa's Dyke blackberrying at an altitude that brought me and my companion eye to eye with the soaring ravens and buzzards as they quartered the valley, and in half a day we gathered five gallons of blackberries. I picked conventionally, but – assessing the quality of fruit as a grade more suitable for wine or jelly than jam – my fellow picker developed a technique of 'milking' bushes, treating each as a black udder from which a stream of juicy pulp must be extracted by an action which began as an embracing grasp and stripped the fruit as his hand constricted it on the downward movement.

The blackberry is a much hybridized plant and it is hard to generalize about patterns of fruiting, but on each cluster of the bush it is usually the lowest berry which ripens first, in

September, and being bigger, juicier and sweeter than any which will follow, it should be eaten fresh. The large cluster is itself composed of smaller bunches of fruit, and again it is the terminal berry on each which now darkens and matures, and it is this secondary harvest late in September which is destined for jams, puddings and pies. By early October the berries which have ripened are small and the pips comprise a greater proportion of the fruit. They should be eaten mixed with apples. By mid-October the harvest is finished and the berries which have been green for a month now darken, but they say the devil has claimed them for his own, for the sweetness has gone.

When you hunt an animal you need to study it, to think the way it thinks, to anticipate its movements. But when you hunt the blackberry you must study your fellow huntsman. This is the most easily found and appreciated fruit of the countryside, so if there is human settlement nearby you must expect competition. There is no special skill required in identifying the fruit or in plucking it, and for this reason it has become a favourite family occupation, as all can contribute to the common pie dish, and each member of the family picks at his own level. The zoning of the bushes which results guides me when I find that I am not the first to have picked them over. My own height makes it natural for me to look for berries hanging between four and five feet from the ground. At this level I am competing with other adults. The adult, knowing the economic value of the crop, being more patient, having a longer reach and being less wary of thorns than a child would be, does a good job of picking. Children are less diligent, become bored quickly, pick in a casual, inefficient way, and strive – if they strive at all – to emulate their parents, reaching where mummy is reaching, always rushing on to the next bush where someone else has found a good crop. I humble myself before a depleted bush, bend the knee, gather what tiny fingers have missed.

But unless you can be the first at the popular picnic spot, it is better to leave it to others. Anywhere with a car park, benches, café, public lavatories – and particularly the new country parks – is known colloquially as a 'honeypot'. Such spots draw the car-borne crowds, leaving the uncharted countryside to those prepared to take it on the country's terms. Look for new territory. Some may be unpromising. A conifer plantation seems a dead spot, but if it is on a south-facing slope, a walk along one of the wide rides designed as a fire-prevention belt can be rewarding, with brambles swarming over the ditch-and-mound boundary. Look too for low-hedged fields which are almost invariably bramble-infested in places.

But primarily, pick for the pleasure of picking. To adopt a cost-benefit-analysis approach in this as in any garnering enterprise is to lose the joy of the action. Tune in to the blackberry, feel that you who seek the berry, and the berry itself as target, are a whole, so that the moment of coming together is like that of the target and the arrow, loosed by the Zen monks at a moment determined by its own rightness, a moment more subtle than any eye–brain co-ordination called 'aiming'. The blackberry is on the bush and you wish to gather it. Don't look for the berry you will pick. Be aware, and find your hand drawn towards berries sensed at the periphery of your vision, as a car driver senses his position relative to one side of the road while keeping his eye focused centrally and far ahead.

My thoughts on the subject are telegraphed ideas, not coherent perhaps but intimating a relationship between the plant and he who gathers from it that cannot fully be explained. Do not ignore one solitary berry which looks worth picking, for on attaining it, unsuspected new vistas of berries open up. When there are many good bushes you may scan one and dismiss it, however, for the whole view of the bush may be a true one.

To many readers I am already raving. Those who are in sympathy with the feelings I express can practise and meditate on Zen in the art of picking blackberries.

The man, the art, the work – it is all one.

The farmer harvests a crop which he knows is there, because he planted it. So the clandestine farmer also goes out in the right season to harvest the crop he has observed, nurtured, maybe even sown. But even when the prospect of one harvest determined the timing of my walk I was aware of the possibilities of other harvests, at present unsuspected, being like Ortega Y Gasset's hunter:

> He does not believe that he knows where the critical moment is going to occur. He does not look tranquilly in one determined direction, sure beforehand that the game will pass in front of him. The hunter knows that he does not know what is going to

happen, and this is one of the greatest attractions of his occupation. Thus he needs to prepare an attention of a different and superior style – an attention which does not consist in riveting itself on the presumed but consists precisely in not presuming anything and in avoiding inattentiveness. It is a 'universal' attention, which does not inscribe itself on any point and tries to be on all points. There is a magnificent term for this, one that still conserves all its zest of vivacity and imminence: alertness. The hunter is the alert man.

Nevertheless, our alertness at the time of harvesting can be aided by experience gained in earlier months. The hazel is not a conspicuous tree – there may be many hidden in hedges and at the fringe of woods which will escape attention in every season but one, and its nuts be observed only by the squirrels in September – but on a fresh morning in January when the hedgerows are free of leaves, each hazel signals its presence by the crimson stigmas of the female flowers which appear among the male catkins. It is a good time to map their presence.

The time to locate the elder is also when it is in flower. Before that moment the tree is best described as nondescript. All praise for the elder is grudgingly bestowed; Richard Mabey writes of the 'mangy, decaying skeletons' of the tree in winter, John Stewart Collis calls it 'that miserable tree' and 'a hopelessly plebeian plant. A bush posing as a tree, a tree failing to be a bush'.

For me the elder's floral advertisement is an annual embarrassment. In constructing tenets of self-sufficiency I find myself including regularly the exhortation 'never go away in June', for this is a month of prodigious activity on the vegetable front, and then a few weeks later, everywhere there are these flower-laden boughs offering the promise of ice-cream soda drinks, fritters and elderflower champagne. I have never devoted sufficient time to mastery of these delights. But in September I am ready for the fruiting; poised on the eve of the season of berries, nuts and fungi, I see the clusters of elder fruit blacken all over and turn down to hang their weighty heads. Each year this is my unfailing harvest, stored below stairs to be enjoyed all winter: bottles of burgundy-like elderberry wine.

The tree is usually small, its branches pliant. You use one hand to bring the fruit within reach, a second to scissor head after head of fruit, a third to hold a vessel in which to catch the falling vintage. Two pairs of hands are therefore best, but somehow I manage alone. Back home, I seek help to shorten an otherwise long task, strigging the fruit by stroking the bunches of berries with a table fork, wide-tined to tug each berry free of its stalk. Many a stalk will fall in the basin, and removing this source of bitterness before it imparts a flavour is what makes the job a little tedious. Some people don't bother. In a poor season, green berries may be numerous, but they float and most can be removed when water is added to make a 'must'. Really ripe heads yield their fruit easily when a fork is pulled through them, but a delicate stroke is needed to free the ripe and leave the green on the stalk.

My most convenient source of elderberries was in my own garden, along its boundary with the farm; and when I wanted more I found them accessible between the arches of Digswell viaduct. I strayed farther afield still in search of blackberries, but it was the farm's resources that particularly attracted me, and so on a Saturday in October, I set off to see what autumn had to offer.

With the corn harvested, the plough had worked its annual transformation, revealing the forms of the earth. The plough strips the land of its old, shabby clothing and leaves it nude. The forms of the ground show like bones beneath the flesh, and each valley has its own valleys separated by ribs of earth. The distant view alone reveals this purity of form; closer, we are rudely made aware of the pores and blisters and stubble of reality – earth torn and turned ready to start the farmer's new year.

I walked along the temple of Lockleys Wood – greying with chalk – a fresh-cut escarpment where the plough had hugged the hedgeline. The Footpath Field, still unploughed, provided me with a short cut to Foxley Grove. I tidied up the Good King Henry patch and retrieved my emergency canister of pyrethrum.

At the start of the walk a shot had turned me away from Whores Wood, where I had planned to go. Now I stayed in Foxley, where the chattering alarm of blackbirds and the battering which the branches received from the wings of woodpigeons as I progressed reassured me that the Forestry Commissioner's ranger was well away. I put up a hen pheasant, which rocketed up and up and up until it seemed her stubby wings could never sustain the impetus of her urgent flight for long enough to clear the canopy.

Hazel-nuts were my immediate goal, though the few I found were dusty and old. But I struck lucky with sweet-chestnuts and discovered that the biggest specimens burst themselves free from their husks in falling, thus sparing me the painful task of splitting them. That evening I roasted a generous batch in front of the fire, slitting all but one which was left to sound a loud warning when its inside was cooked. But it failed to explode and the remainder overcooked with it and were burnt to a cinder . . . Fortunately I had plenty more.

On 19 October I had two small puffballs sliced and fried with my breakfast bacon, but they had virtually no taste. Next time I found them, I tried stewing the puffballs in milk, the most mucilaginous dish imaginable, somewhat like tripe. I conjured them up in my mind as 'spook's eyeballs' which didn't help. Worse, the next item on the menu was chestnut soup, puréed and served in milk. Very sickly. Supper hung heavy on my stomach, culinary experience hard won . . .

The trouble with all my gleaning from the wild was that initially I was eating it in parallel with a conventional diet, and was rarely hungry enough to make any dish of debatable merit really acceptable. Hunger dulls the critical faculties, but my tests were really testing. Anything that tastes good to a well-fed taster must be good.

There is no denying that I had many disappointments, both from food that failed to live up to its inflated reputation, and more from the crops that failed to materialize. Such a one was walnuts.

Starting from an historical clue, my enthusiasm grew as I read about *Juglans regia*. It had been cultivated in the British Isles since the fifteenth century, but like the sweet-chestnut tree its seedlings cannot be expected to give good quality nuts when they mature. Selected cultivars, budded or grafted, are essential. And I had it from local historian Branch Johnson that walnuts had been introduced to Lockleys 300 or so years ago. Could it not be that the trained gardening staff working at the manor house might have grafted new specimens to replace those grown too old to fruit well?

Edward Wingate of Lockleys was an MP for St Albans who fought for the Parliamentary forces in the Civil War and who died at Lockleys in 1634. 'It was his son Edward who established there a famous warren of silver-haired rabbits and "a great store of excellent walnut trees" – the name of the Warren and many walnut trees remain today,' Branch Johnson recorded in 1960. I didn't find the walnut trees, planted to feed gamebirds and no doubt for the most part felled in the First World War to make walnut butts for Lee-Enfield rifles, but as so often happens on an outing of this kind, I found something else by way of consolation.

On Saturday 20 October I set out on an overcast afternoon with rain forecast, in search of walnuts. A clockwise circumnavigation of the farm took me first to the big sweet-chestnut by the farm fence in our neighbour's garden. There were no nuts to be found – the leaf fall under a chestnut effectively carpets the ground, obscuring everything – but overall this had been the only worthwhile chestnut I had discovered on the farm that autumn. (Sadly, the next year it yielded nothing but skinny husks. As Richard Jefferies said, 'No tree is apparently so capricious in its yield as the chestnut in English woods.') Turning at the corner of the ploughed fields, I started picking up acorns: the first good fall of acorns I had seen that year. Later I was leaching the tannin out of some and grinding ersatz corn, and roasting others to determine what kind of coffee-type beverage they make (not as good as dandelion, I decided).

Farther along the hedge I dug out a dandelion root for roasting, using my sheath knife, and then about six cuckoo-pint roots. Each cuckoo-pint had a stem with red berries, but it came away from the earth at a touch, having rotted through at the base of the stem. I dug down at the point where each had been standing and found there the white root corms, most of them with a shoot descending. I left the smaller ones, taking only the fatter specimens for baking to neutralize the poison which gives the plant its bad reputation. Sir Hugh Platt writing in 1596 in his 'Sundrie new and Artificiall remedies against famine, written . . . vppon thoccasion of this present Dearth' said you can make 'excellent bread of the roots of Aaron called Cuckow pit or starch rootes'.

The same plant, also called lords-and-ladies, grew

prolifically in the shadier parts of my garden, and when I transplanted it into well-tilled and -fed soil the multiplication of the roots was impressive, so I wasn't worried about threatening the species.

The starch-filled corm, in common with the rest of the plant, contains a poison compounded of an alkaloid, which is akin to coniine (the active constituent of hemlock), together with saponin and calcium oxalate. A surprising number of food plants require preliminary treatment to eliminate their poisonous principle, but the knowledge of how to render the food safe is so well established as to be taken for granted. Schoolchildren may hesitate before eating tapioca pudding, but surely not on the grounds that the parent plant – cassava, a staple food in the tropics – contains prussic acid? After drying or boiling, the root is made harmless. And so it was with cuckoo-pint, many years ago, when after treatment it was sold as Portland sago or arrowroot. The industry is now almost forgotten, even on the Isle of Portland, where it was based. At the time of the first Queen Elizabeth, the tubers were also used to produce a very white starch which was greatly esteemed in the laundries of the day.

The disadvantage of the starch was that the oxalate crystals reddened the hands of the laundresses, but there was apparently no similar drawback to the arrowroot. The tubers were dug in July or August and the offsets were replanted. After the roots had been washed the fibres and skin were rubbed off, and the bulk was pounded to a pulp in a mortar. The pulp was washed in a sieve, pounded again, and stood under water for twenty-four hours. Then with the water changed, it was given another day's soaking. The water was discarded and the remaining solids were dried and stored in paper bags in a dry place. No metal utensils were used with Arum root. When I tried it, I found this process straightforward, although the first pulping was a slippery business!

I carried on along the hedgerow towards the apex of a wooded triangle, where the field-edge path began to diverge from the course of the road. The hedge dwindled until it was nothing more than the bushing of epicormic shoots from the boles of elm trees, and there in among tussocky grass and dead leaves I saw a clump of shaggy parasol toadstools. I had my field guide to fungi with me and checked the identification points, noting the unmarked stem which principally differentiates between this species and the parasol which grows in the open. But they are equally good eating. I picked them and put them in my haversack. A little farther on I saw another clump just over the railings which marked the boundary with Sherrardswood School. I picked these too, making a collection sufficient for several meals, for the heads of the largest were three or four inches across. Once over the fence I was trespassing on new ground, ornamental woods laid out around Lockleys, and the most likely place to find the elusive walnut. I saw no walnut tree, but only more shaggy parasol.

It was a long walk that day, and I augmented my fungus haul with a few puffballs picked in the open rides of Lockleys Wood. That evening I fried both puffballs and a few of the parasol mushrooms in butter and ate them with a saveloy from the fried fish shop. My wife tried the parasol and commented that they tasted the way mushrooms used to taste. A cultivated mushroom would be very insipid in comparison with this robust flavour.

When I went out again on 27 October the leaves were falling fast and made me wonder what they concealed. In the open clearings of coppiced woodland the brown drifts covered the ground like dun snow, and finding fungi – like finding sweet-chestnuts – was much more difficult, save for two specimens which grew prolifically in Foxley Grove, sulphur tuft and a dark-centred brown fungus. (Later I decided these were one of the clitocybes or lactarius, and as neither they nor the sulphur tuft are for eating, the difficulty in identification was more in the nature of frustration than loss.)

Identifying fungi is difficult. None of the specimens I brought home bore any resemblance to the plates in the guide. I abandoned it and bought a new one, the Collins *Guide to Mushrooms and Toadstools*, but it was still difficult. However, I was optimistic. I knew that in 1915 Sir Edward Salisbury had published the results of his classic ecological study of the oak–hornbeam woods of Hertfordshire in two issues of the *Journal of Ecology*. If I had a check list of the fungi he found growing in these habitats it would at least let me know what to look for. Sixty years ago the woods were coppiced in rotation for a wood crop, and the range of flora to be encountered now would certainly be restricted, as the uncoppiced woods attained a climax of growth. Nevertheless I felt sure E. J. Salisbury would offer the best information available. I ordered the relevant journals from the library.

The treatise, seventy-seven pages long, distils an incredible total of tirelessly accumulated ecological evidence. I read it through, thinking that if I worked hard enough at the subject, one day I would be able fully to appreciate the range of information supplied. Little of it was directly useful to me, but in a section headed 'The Cryptogamic Flora' in Part Two, I thought I would find what I was searching for.

The oak–hornbeam woods here are of two kinds, depending on whether the oak standards are common oaks or sessile oaks. Ours are common, having a long acorn stalk (the sessile acorn is stalkless), and Salisbury reports that in woods including the common oak, in the well-drained chalk zones of the county 'the cryptogamic flora . . . appears to be distinctly poor compared with that of the Quercus sessiliflora–Carpinus woods in the same area' in which, he later remarks, over 450 species of fungi have been observed. This was a blow, because I hoped to make a great deal of fungi as a free food resource. But more annoying still was the note that 'the fungi are under investigation at the hands of Mr J. Ramsbottom, MA, so that no list is here given.'

I knew of Dr John Ramsbottom by reputation. In 1950 he retired after forty years' service in the Department of Botany at the Natural History Museum, having been Keeper of Botany for twenty years. He had just begun that service when Edward Salisbury was carrying out his oak–hornbeam research. *Mushrooms and Toadstools* is John Ramsbottom's classic. I ordered a copy, and when it arrived, turned to the chapter on woodlands. It contains lists of species likely to be found in almost every kind of woodland. Oak woods, he says, 'have not so many characteristic species as beech woods, but there are a few species of Boletus, though none of them is common'. Of hornbeams he says nothing. I felt completely deflated. The explanation was to be found in the author's preface, where he said that the book 'when first written greatly exceeded the required length'! The manuscript actually had to be reduced by half, and the chapter on woodlands and another 'are but shadows of their former selves'.

So all the hopes I had built up through having had two eminent natural historians research in detail the very terrain on which I was foraging, were dashed. I leaned heavily thereafter on 'fungus forays' organized by the local history society, and was reassured by one expert from the British Museum that I need have no qualms about extinguishing the species when I picked a full crop of fungi, as they were only the fruiting body. The plant itself remained secure underground. He also reminded me that when I opened a tin of mushroom soup, one thing I could be sure not to find inside was a mushroom. 'If it had mushroom in it, it would cost four times as much and probably be less tasty,' he said, and explained that commercial soup-makers used *Boletus edulis*, the fungus the French call *cep.* Unfortunately the foray always occurred on Mardley Heath, which although containing some stretches of oak–hornbeam, was very mixed woodland with a great deal of birch. This always yielded a high fungus count, but little that I encountered on my home ground. Nevertheless, Boletus was well represented, and in addition to *Boletus edulis*, other members of the family make good eating.

Ramsbottom remarks with satisfaction on 'a more general realization that many toadstools may be eaten with perfect safety and can add a spice of variety to diets requiring only this to make them satisfying'.

My hauls were usually large, and I preferred to dry the surplus rather than over-indulge. So I was pleased to note that 'dried, *Boletus edulis* and the cultivated mushroom are richer in protein than any dried vegetable except nuts'.

One day I returned to Mardley Heath to see what kind of a Boletus haul I could make, and returned with half a dozen large specimens. I failed to identify them individually, but the sponge-like gills make genus identification positive, so I kept them all. Some of the books advise you to strip the sponge layer away and discard it, while others say it is edible. I had discovered the year before that the stalks are tough eating, and I learned then not to wash the Boletus crop either – mine had been grubby, so I washed them, and the sponge sucked up water like butter on a hot crumpet. This time I merely picked them over to remove bits of dead leaf. The skin of the fungus cap is the principal site of its varied mineral constituents, and should only be peeled if it is badly soiled.

I had a recipe I wanted to try, for lentil and mushroom stew, but when the Boletus was ready it fell somewhat short of the weight required. I had some dried Boletus left from the previous year, prepared at the same time as my shaggy parasol harvest. I had tried drying them all on trays standing on the boiler, until my wife found maggots dropping out and ordered them out of the kitchen. I finished them off in front of a hot radiator and they had been stored away ever since. I also had a packet of *cep* which I had bought in a *charcuterie* in Boulogne in the summer, and remembered the emphatic advice of the shopkeeper to reconstitute them '*de l'eau chaude*'. I warmed the water and dropped the hardened, black strips of Boletus in, watching them swell to their original proportions. Drained, they made up the required eight ounces, and I set to work to prepare the stew, adding carrots and celery from the garden. When it was done, it looked to be more sustaining than appetizing . . . I christened it Fungus Glop and delved in the half-gallon saucepan with a wooden spoon for some of the Boletus, which I sampled cautiously before tipping the lot into a bowl to cool down. My idea was to freeze it all in the morning. And so to bed.

In the night I dreamed of toadstools, and waking could think of nothing else as I lay in bed, going over in my mind the time I had read that it is not the poisonous fungi that make people ill so much as the poor putrefying specimens of otherwise edible fungi which they cannot bring themselves to reject.

On reflection I decided my gathered Boletus had left something to be desired, and recalled that the dried stock had been stored in a damp room in a jar which might not have been airtight. I was late getting up and then I got the runs as I have never had them before. I paid five visits to the wc before I left the house, but I said nothing to my wife or the children. I couldn't. I knew that the years of example would never result in them actually sharing the food I brought home if their fears of being poisoned were substantiated in any way.

My breakfast was served: liver and bacon. I managed it, but there was a greater ordeal ahead. The fast freeze was switched on, and there stood the basin of fungus glop, hard-skinned now it was cold: turgid, turdified. The plan was to measure it in two-cup portions into plastic bags which in turn would stand in boxes to freeze in large cubes. I began to ladle the muck in. If I could have done it cleanly I might have been all right, but I kept finding it spilling at the bag openings. Now the worst stage was at hand. We were all hurrying that morning. No one could spare time to help me. The air had to be evacuated from the bags using a straw before the tops were twist-fastened. I did two, inhaling the smell with my face just inches from the offensive concoction. And then I could do no more. I ran upstairs and retched with my head over the bathroom basin.

All day I felt weak, but at lunchtime I managed to eat cold meat, chutney and a baked potato. I went to bed at nine and the next day felt better. The glop was frozen, but what was to become of it? I searched through a book of medical advice for travellers to confirm a friend's suggestion, that my attack had come too soon after the tasting for the Boletus to have precipitated it. And yet what else could it have been? What had I eaten the previous day which could have upset me? Nothing that I could recall. I had eaten just one large meal, with a little wine, and that had been at the Council Chairman's Civic Ball . . .

On Thursday 7 November, my wife was out all day so I returned at lunchtime and ate half a pint of 'lentil and mushroom stew'. I found it tasty, but the pleasure was marred by my concern at the possible after-effects. But in fact my health remained good. The next day I came across an entry in *Food for Free* in which Richard Mabey warns the reader specifically against eating the species of Boletus which is stippled red. One of mine might have been; so now I worried again, that the dramatic effect of eating fungus glop might depend on the gamble of whether you happened to have a stippled bit in your bowl. Could I ever be sure of the three pints that remained? I didn't sample it again for a while, and then, when my mother was staying with us for a few days, my wife suggested that 'we have some of your stuff . . .' That really had me worried. Without liking the strategy, I had to admit that it was astute. My wife would know I wouldn't let my mother eat anything dubious, while she feared I would take greater risks with the family. This was surely a test of my confidence. And how confident was I? Again I felt that too much was at stake for me to admit reservations over the wholesomeness of the fungus glop. Here indeed was the opportunity I needed. If I was prepared for my mother to eat it, then at least I would have my wife and children trying their first main fungus dish. With an air of confident bravado I joined the family at table to discover before me a bowl of celery and tomato soup, part of a batch I had made from garden vegetables and frozen down weeks before. All along, this was the 'stuff' which had been intended.

I have now consumed all the glop, eating it alone for lunch or supper, and never suffering from any after-effect. It is a kind of progress. But I would like to know if anyone else had the runs the day after the Civic Ball . . .

What standards of quality should the clandestine farmer observe? It is sensible to be wary of the process of decay, to observe the warning of Dr E. V. McCollum, to eat only those foods that spoil, or rot or decay, but eat them before they do. But if you demand the immaculate appearance that food has in the supermarket, you will go hungry.

Appearance is not always a good guide to the value of food. The fruit and vegetables we bring in from our own back gardens and appreciate for their freshness and flavour might very well be passed over by the housewife in a greengrocers: too much mud on it (which, though increasing the weight on the scales, may be less harmful than traces of detergent on a washed potato), tine-scarred, pecked by birds.

We are competing for our food plants with a host of other animals and insects, and one solution is to surprise the early bird by an even earlier uprising and be first at the harvest. Another is to share the harvest and be as philosophical about the peck-marked apple as one was about the bullfinch who thinned out the blossom in the spring. Better still is to watch the predator, to see who shares your predilections, and when he has grown fat, eat him. This is certainly the logical way to tackle the problem of rabbits and pigeons: to treat them as liberated domestic animals, freer than free-range, but destined for the pot. Other more lowly predators can also provide a meal, as I was to discover.

It is enough to demand that food from the countryside should be fresh. To have it looking perfect means that either we must exclude the pests which compete for it, or we must poison them. The organic gardeners take a cheerfully philosophic view when they bite into an apple and find a maggot. Well, they say, if *he* wasn't poisoned then *we* should be all right.

I acknowledge that I must eat many larvae in the course of a year, and although I am put off once their presence is revealed, I rarely stop to hunt. Larvae and enzymes begin the process of decay. Bacteria will follow, and soon the food will be putrid. Moulds may liberate one of a hundred kinds of hazardous metabolites, such as the toxic aflatoxins.

Decay is a vital part of the earth's life cycle even when it competes with your own needs. We put it to good use on our compost heap, when the destructive action of bacteria fixes nitrogen from the air within the humus that will return new life to the soil. The changes are complex, the chain immense. A succession of some 200 fungus species accomplish the recycling of a cow pat in the meadow, while 500–600 effect the destruction of wood. These scavenging agencies perform a vital role, but we must hold them in check at times or we will starve when fresh food is in short supply. Some food must be preserved, but always it is better that it be eaten fresh. It demands a discipline, to eat always what is available, not necessarily what you fancy at that moment. The shops know our weakness. They stock everything we want, preserved in some way, to be ready always whenever we want it. We can stock up our cupboards, and relax, safe in the knowledge that the next meal, and the one after, are waiting for us. After all, it is only by securing a surplus that we can buy time for pursuits that are not directly inspired by the need to survive. A purse full of housekeeping money is the modern equivalent of Aladdin's lamp, and there's a cave full of treasure in every High Street – the supermarket.

To a primitive people, the ability to accumulate and preserve all the foods needed to sustain life would have inspired religious awe. It is easy to forget that for many people even today, acquiring food or earning the money to pay for it, is their major task in life. An average consumer in a developing country will spend over 60 per cent of his income on food. In America, at the other extreme, the figure is only 16 per cent. The ready supply of food at a reasonable price increases leisure and is a cornerstone of civilization.

But the supermarket as Aladdin's cave and source of all nourishment has gone too far in the way of making dreams come true, for the grocer's own logistical problems of transport, of shelf life, of refrigeration, of cosmetic colouring and packaging to ensure eye appeal, and double wrapping to preserve crispness have distorted and distended the natural food chain – which should lead from the earth to the mouth by the shortest path in terms both of time and distance if the energy equation is to remain sane. Now we may find ourselves preserving whole crops that should ideally be eaten fresh. Even in a country district where everyone sees consumable food growing all around them, hardly any part of it will end up in their larder. All will go to be distributed and redistributed on a national, even an international scale. Common sense tells me that if freshness is the factor that enables me to enjoy most food at its optimum of flavour and goodness then local production for local consumption is the easiest way to achieve it. If some city dwellers have to put up with food that is several days old, that is the price they pay for leaving the country. But surely we need not all pay the same price, particularly when the introduction of chemical additives is a suspect art?

If you are hungry and there is fresh food to hand, then eat the food while it is fresh. There then remain just three good reasons for preserving a proportion of the food that is available to you: (1) there may be a glut of a particular crop, when preserving it becomes the only practical way of avoiding waste; (2) even if a crop in season is not so heavy that you cannot consume it all, it may be better not to over-indulge – preserving part of the crop so as to spread consumption over a longer period helps us to a better balanced diet; (3) preserved food is provision for the proverbial 'rainy day', lessening the blow of the harvest that fails, filling the hungry gap between the fruits of the autumn and the first spring shoots.

These are the reasons why I dry, freeze, salt, pickle, ferment and bottle my produce as food and drink. You feel a special affinity with the store cupboard when you have personally been involved with the food at every stage of its preservation. But beware the desire to lay *everything* down. There's only one best time to eat today's food and that's today.

# 8 The bracken battle

While the hunting was being done for me by the foxes, I concentrated on becoming a more effective farmer. Always the question was how to help my crops prosper while a more dominant form of vegetation survived. Could I keep the bracken in check? More research was called for and in my second year as a clandestine farmer I started on it.

Cutting the bracken as it appeared offered only a short-term solution, for I suspected that new shoots would continue to appear, and I would be faced with a burden of weeding which would never be lightened unless the bracken were killed off in some way. It went counter to my philosophy to turn to herbicides, for I saw clandestine farming as a move away from inorganic technology, and I knew of no country lore that would help. So I turned to books – and found an answer in Darlington's *Natural History Atlas of Great Britain.*

> Although notoriously difficult to control, it [bracken] can be killed off if its fronds are cut off at ground level three times a year when in the 'asparagus' stage (i.e. while they are still elongating but before the pinnae and pinnules have unfurled).

As soon as I had read that, I gained confidence which was to keep my enthusiasm soaring high well into the second summer. I had the land, I had a good annual crop which was apparently seeding well, and now I had a simple formula to wrest the land from the present colonizer.

In that second spring I learnt some more good news. In my own garden I found fresh shoots emerging from where each of the Good King Henry plants had died down. I put it down to the mild winter, then went to the reference books and found that only the one I had first consulted gave the plant as an annual. Everywhere else it was a perennial! I went back to the farm to see how it fared there. My plot was marked by grass where I had kept the bracken down, and beyond that lay bent, brown fronds. There was little sign of emergent shoots on my first two inspections of the old Good King Henry plants, but on 31 March I noted that the shoots of those I could find were about one inch out of the ground. Two weeks later I was able to locate five growing plants, and I chopped away at the bluebell growth which now looked a bigger threat than bracken, until I realized a scythe would be a more sensible tool than a sheath knife.

The following week-end I returned armed with the head of a rake, and a cheap hand fork concealed in my jacket. I carried a rough ash pole, one end of which had been whittled down to make a snug fit into the rake's socket. Once inside Foxley Grove I assembled this clandestine tool, used a rock to bang in a retaining nail, and began the task of raking dead bracken off the vegetable patch, so that I could the better sever new shoots as they emerged. On the southerly edge of the wood some bracken was in full frond, but I found that even after the dead plants were removed I still needed to probe into the humus to find the buds, which were just below the surface. I worked circumspectly, because it was a fearful morning, with a Landrover passing repeatedly along the perimeter of the wood and snatches of voices heard without my being able to locate the source of the sounds.

On my next visit I heard a dog bark and had to restrain the impulse to leave the wood and return to the footpath; I held my ground. It was very clearly my ground to anyone who had chanced on it, because the stems of the bluebells showed blanched white where I had cut them. By the end of April the bluebells were out all over the wood, and they stayed in flower, getting better and better all the time until the middle of May, a purple-blue haze at the foot of the trees. They made a good cover for the advance of the bracken. By 4 May I was noting bracken 'fiddleheads' a foot high amongst the flowers, and to ensure that they were cut before they unfurled I scythed the whole plot, and scythed two other clearings I had located higher up the hill to act as reserve allotments in case I had to abandon the first. The cuckoo arrived now to make his inevitable comment on the proceedings . . .

The crescendo of colour in the woods was matched on the meadow slope I crossed at the beginning and end of each farming trip, a picture painted in green, white and yellow. Lush grass set off the yellow spots of buttercup and cowslip, with drifts of white cow-parsley blossom at the top of the hill. And I was seeing a lot of this hill, as the business of following the bracken-cutting formula began to dominate my leisure.

I had hoped that if I made three cuts with one week between them, the job would be done, but now I realized it was not going to be anything like as simple as the formula made it sound. The time between the emergence of the shoot and the breaking out of the first leaf fronds is relatively brief. How did you set about cutting the fronds three times a year when in the 'asparagus' stage, if they were all emerging at different times? To catch any individual frond before it was too late meant twice-weekly cutting sessions. I began to wonder also whether it meant that each individual shoot had to be severed on three separate occasions. If so, I couldn't cut them at ground level or I would never find them to make another cut. I was further confused by learning that 'cutting two or three times a year for two or three successive seasons has proved a very successful method of control' of bracken: a summary in his book *Weeds and Aliens* by Sir Edward Salisbury of an article published in 1935.

Unsure now about how much work I had let myself in for, I resolved to do the best I could. I chopped bracken on 12 May, 16 May, 20 May, 24 May and then on 28 May. Far from being eliminated, on that last visit I counted *600* stems sliced through with my knife before I grew bored with counting, and then went on to cut at least 100 more. Where I had raked, the shoots were easy to see. Elsewhere they were elusive, but in failing light they showed up a pale green against the surrounding vegetation. Clearly the checks to its growth which I had administered the previous year had served to stimulate the plant rather than weaken it.

From then on I began to keep a regular tally of scalps taken from my hydra-headed foe. On 2 June it reach 544. By 8 June, 400 more had emerged, and were duly levelled. On 16 June the tally was down to 300 and the shoots were now coming up thin and straggly. I wrote in my notebook: 'Is this the beginning of the end?' Next time, 24 June, it was down again, 200. 'They are coming up spindlier now,' I wrote, 'but still they come up.' This time I used a scythe. The pollen count was high, and suffering as I do from hay fever I was blocked with mucus as I worked, a sodden handkerchief around my face, covering my mouth and nose.

I was determined that there should be sufficient plants to take over the areas I cleared, but to my disappointment the second season's sowing of Good King Henry failed to germinate for the most part, and I had just a few seedlings in the cold frame. Around my oldest plant in the garden, however, a mass of seedlings was coming up. The ground pattern was fascinating, an elongated arrowhead pointing down wind from the parent plant. As the seedlings grew larger I transplanted them into seed boxes, and when they were big enough to plant out early in June, I took them over to the farm. What particularly pleased me was the way the established plant had produced hundreds of viable seeds. If the plants on the farm would do this, I would be not so much encouraging them in future as thinning them out!

On 30 June I went to the cold frame and looked at the few Good King Henry seedlings which I had grown from the packet. At once I recognized the goosefoot shape of the mature leaf. The self-sown seedlings didn't look like this at all! They must be some entirely different plant. And then I remembered. The year before, I had made it a rule to allow one of every weed species that germinated in my vegetable garden to grow to maturity so that I could make a positive identification from the flower. Two of the plants were nightshades, and I let the plants stay long enough for the berries to ripen so that I could identify one with confidence as woody nightshade and the other as deadly nightshade. Then I pulled them up. But not soon enough, it seemed. I had carefully transplanted two or three dozen plants of deadly nightshade into Foxley Grove and sweated as I carried gallons of water to irrigate their young roots and do what I could to establish them on my three plots! Somewhat despondent now, I carried the real Good King Henry over to the farm. The bracken was waiting for me. And for the first time the numbers were up. I cut 278 sprouts. On 8 July I returned and scored 584, the second highest tally of the summer.

Looking back on those weeks now, I can't imagine why I did not feel in a black humour, but my diary was not dominated by the unending struggle to win a clearing. That last visit was on a lovely evening. Because I favoured the cloak that rain gave to my activities I had forgotten how beautiful it was in the sunshine on the meadow. The purple of hardhead and fragrant orchid were dominant where they grew, but the grass was so high in places that it was difficult to follow the path. Ladybirds poised delicately on slender stems, and a massive flock of sparrows rose from the stiff green wheat of the Bottom Park field as I disturbed them. I heard a grasshopper and the nostalgia of youthful summers dimly recollected flooded over me.

The established Good King Henry looked lean and dry, in need of rain. On my return walk I found three wild strawberry plants laden with fruit. I had never seen so many ripe at one time. I picked about thirty strawberries and carried them home in my hand. I shared them with my younger son, Christopher, and we thought them very good.

On 15 July I set out with some sense of urgency, because it was likely to be two or three weeks before next I could make this walk. It had been raining all day, and although it was a fine evening now, there were rainclouds scudding across the sky so I wore a waterproof jacket and over-trousers. The grass on the meadow wasn't as high as it had been, but the rain beating it down had further obscured the path. Incongruously I carried the obligatory gallon of water. As I crossed the barley field, the musty, dusty aroma of the harvest arose from the grain, despite the damping down it had had. Almost without emotion I noted the new flush of bracken shoots on my plot in the wood, and I cut, and cut, and cut, a total of 452 sprouts and fronds.

There was a two-week interval. The corn looked golden when next I walked across the farm, and I stripped a handful of wheat berries into my hand, threshing and winnowing them between my palms. The grain was tasty, but still soft to chew on. In the woods the ground beneath my feet was tinder dry; flaking dried leaves and the crunchy shells of bluebell seed made it feel as though I was walking over a great dry bowl of breakfast cereal. As I emerged from the trees and looked over my plot an unbelievable green sea of bracken fronds and hemp nettle confronted me. I looked for Good King Henry plants and found two, before I left, disheartened. In my notebook I wrote 'experiment abandoned', and added a phrase from Thoreau, 'Enjoy the land but own it not.'

At that moment I had a clear enough vision of what the future might hold for me: intensive husbandry to achieve a viable crop and reasonable return for my labour, all of which would increase my attachment to this particular plot and make me resent any intrusion on it. All the arguments for enclosure of common land were clearer than they had ever been. If wresting a crop from the soil was this difficult on unenclosed land, in what way did it offer an alternative to agriculture at any level of subsistence?

What persuaded me to continue, despite all the doubts that failure had awakened, was a growing conviction that my failure stemmed from ignorance, that there existed a fund of knowledge, once part of the common peasant culture, an oral tradition of subsistence among Goldsmith's 'bold peasantry, their country's pride' which 'once destroyed can never be supplied'. The peasantry had been destroyed, but much of the culture remained in libraries, or was being recreated through scientific research. I diligently began to tap it.

I learned that my choice of Good King Henry as a food staple was perhaps misguided, because its oxalic acid content can be responsible for symptoms of iron and calcium deficiency even when apparently adequate amounts of these minerals are included in the diet. Oxalic acid has the effect of locking up the calcium and iron in Good King Henry, and stealing more besides from other foods, so that the minerals are not available to the body. Spinach contains almost 1 per cent of oxalic acid, and Lawrence Hills has said that 'the child who will not eat up his spinach is wiser than his parents'. But of all the plants he lists as being rich in oxalic acid (the constituent which makes rhubarb leaves poisonous), the richest is the much vaunted edible weed Fat Hen, *Chenopodium album*, a close relative of Good King Henry. 'It is the oxalic acid that handicaps the order *Chenopodiaceae* as good vegetables, and it will be seen that though they are high in calcium they take it all away again and more,' says Mr Hills in *Grow Your Own Fruit and Vegetables*.

Those words set me off in search of a new wild plant, but I did this with enthusiasm rather than pessimism, because I had learned far more about bracken by now – and my new knowledge gave me confidence, plus a new moral fervour.

Initially all predatory acts against wild plants offended my conservationist principles, though I clung to exclusion clauses, such as the motive of providing an economic crop, given as one reason for species introductions in the pamphlet *Policy on Introduction to Nature Reserves.* But bracken is in a different class, as it poses a threat to other species – apparently including man. In addition to becoming the dominant plant in its environment, shading all other ground flora, it has been shown by Dr I. A. Evans and her colleagues at Bangor to contain carcinogens which can possibly be transferred to humans through the medium of milk and water. 'The findings from Bangor should serve to encourage a mass campaign to eradicate bracken from our grazing lands, let alone the moorland and other habitats on which it has encroached so much,' wrote Bruce Campbell in a crusading article.

The only way to kill bracken by cultivation is to exhaust the food stocks which the plant holds in its underground rhizomes. 'The secret of success lies in the systematic destruction of the fronds until the plant is starved to death. A cessation of cutting is comparable to leaving a forest fire smouldering,' warned K. W. Braid, after he had described in the *Scottish Journal of Agriculture* the labyrinthine underground system which supports the surface growth. A single plant may extend for dozens of square yards and produce hundreds of fronds. The leader rhizome, which is the principal invader of new territory, will be one or two feet underground, with branches rising from it to occupy a parallel stratum at a depth of about nine inches. There may be ten feet of rhizomes below each square foot of surface, and estimates of the total weight of rhizome under an acre of brake vary between ten and fifty tons, and it is all packed with food reserves. Braid recommends two or more cuttings for the first year or two with an interval of five to six weeks between cuts, and warns that it will be a minimum of three years before the plant dies, and possibly more than five.

'During the second year the number of fronds produced is sometimes greater than in the previous year, but they are considerably smaller and by the third year there is a noteworthy decrease in number and in size.'

In June to July the fronds are fully grown and have drained rhizome food reserves to the maximum without having begun to contribute significant amounts of replacement food. Cut at this moment they are less likely to be replaced by new shoots than is the case when the 'fiddleheads' are severed, although their stems have hardened. In sum, the moment when I wrote in my diary 'experiment abandoned' was precisely the time when I should have laid in with a scythe to level all! As it was, I had given the bracken a whole summer to recuperate. But I learned too that the plant needs its thick top dressing of dead fronds through the winter to protect the higher levels of rhizomes from frost damage. I resolved to deprive the plant of this insulation layer in time for the worst of the winter. The battle was on again!

# 9 The woods

Heat is the last gift of the tree, freely released when the timber is no longer useful in any other way; but for the clandestine farmer gleaning in the woods, the tree's last gift is likely to be the first he enjoys. I began writing this chapter in the winter, sitting in the front room of the cottage I rent for my work from Taylor's of Welwyn, who make beehives; warmed by a small Norwegian wood-burning stove, the Jøtul 602. Each morning I stacked it with deal off-cuts from the joinery, and if this first free source of fuel failed me, I brought in hornbeam logs. With the damper closed, the wood burns like a cigar, and I could boil a saucepan on the hot plate and bake potatoes in foil just inside the fire-door.

At night I would go home and spend the evening before an open fire extravagantly and inefficiently burning big hornbeam logs which we had sawn and split in the garden on frosty weekend mornings when only logging would keep you warm. I was lucky to have so much wood freely available. When it has gone I will go on gleaning from the woods, where there is enough to keep me supplied for years in return for the effort of portage. When I see the cost of coal and gas, oil and electricity, I am surprised that none of my neighbours takes a walk up to the woods on a winter's day with a stout cord in his pocket to loop around a bundle of dead wood. Perhaps they would, if they had not had the chimney blocked off when the central heating went in.

Such self-granted rights are those of fire-bote and house-bote, as the Early English claimed them, or estovers, derived from the Norman-French *estouffer* – 'to furnish'. Hence the common right of cutting and taking tree loppings, or gorse, furze, bushes, underwood, heather or fern, off a common for fuel to burn in the commoner's house or for the repair of house and farm buildings, hedges, fences and farm implements.

Such rights are wide open to abuse, but in an overcrowded world what ventures are not? Where the actions of one person prevent another from enjoying a subordinate right, then the first comer needs to exercise restraint. Freedom in my catechism is a far cry from licence. The meaning was well taken by H. A. Williams when he wrote, 'Freedom is not so much a right, still less is it a luxury. It is a duty and a burden, the cross we have to carry if we want to be fully human.'

If everyone had open fires we would need to extend the smoke abatement ordinances beyond the towns. They do not reach to where I live, but I will respect them if they come, for they are a social advance, good community practice, enabling all to breathe more freely. My bit of smoke meanwhile does little harm, certainly no more than the far more wasteful bonfire.

What concerns me more is the threat to the countryside which could accompany a new recognition of the value of wood. One instance was reported while this book was being written:

> People trying to beat the fuel crisis are ravaging woodlands at Livingston New Town, West Lothian, where more than 500,000 trees have been planted over the past eight years.
>
> Birches and oaks have been felled and other trees ripped out by the roots. Mr Malcolm Drummond, the corporation's forestry and landscape officer, said: 'Some trees have been felled just for the sake of a few easily cut branches for firewood.' (*Daily Telegraph*, 5 March 1974).

The scale of society blinds the uneducated and they fail to see that what they destroy is theirs. A culture scaled to human proportions might breed a race of foragers like the New Forest commoners who once all claimed rights of turbary, and stripped the turf layer for fuel, but knew the rule of 'take one and leave two' so that the turf gash would grow over more quickly.

When rights are formalized it is possible to rule at which point abuse begins. Here in Hertfordshire there is a common where right of estovers may still be exercised by householders of the parish. This is on the 240 acres of Aldbury Common which lies on the county's boundary with Buckinghamshire. In 1937, the Aldbury Parish Council reached an agreement with the National Trust, as owners of the Ashridge Estate, that the householders of the parish were entitled to common of pasture, and to the cutting of fern and gorse and the taking of chalk, and fallen wood up to nine inches in diameter.

I spent a day out at Aldbury looking into the history of the common rights, then walking through the woods with the Clerk to the Parish Council, Mr Percy Crow, while he exercised them. To be honest, on this occasion it was something of a token act, but to my great satisfaction we saw two people up there carrying bow saws and with branches over their shoulders, and on our return journey by car passed a pedestrian parishioner bearing a bag packed with logs.

By defining the available wood as 'fallen' and 'up to nine inches in diameter' the Aldbury agreement defends both the growing timber and, providentially, the larger fallen trunks which provide a specialized ecological enclave for fungi, crane flies and beetles.

Just to confuse the issue, there is a good conservationist case to be made for cutting the living timber in a controlled way, and leaving all the dead wood where it lies, for it is becoming another scarce biological resource and needs to be preserved as a vital component of the forest. There is no particular virtue in cleaning up the ground litter of decaying wood brought down by the last high wind, and where forests are tidied up in this way it is usually because of an authority's 'visual amenity policy' and simply adds a further item to the cost of management. It has been claimed that the removal of fallen timber and decaying trees could reduce the varieties of fauna of the natural forest by as many as a fifth of the total. A small piece of dead wood the size of your arm may provide a home for fifty species. In one survey, 231 species were found in association with three-inch logs on the ground. The chains are complex and interrelated. Up to fifty species may depend on the presence and activity of one kind of bark beetle.

This is not the place for an impassioned defence of organisms with which the layman can detect no economic link. Suffice it to say that the 'genetic pool' may provide economic riches in the same way that the drug penicillin – first found in a mould – proved mercifully efficacious in the field of medicine. The most humble-seeming organism is a link in the chain that runs through nature. Break a link and the result can be catastrophic. You could not admire a flower were it not for the agents of decay that transform dead matter above and below ground level into plant-nourishing humus.

In broadleaf forest the fungi and insects associated with dead wood are in most cases only able to attack unhealthy or dead timber so they pose no risk to the healthy tree. It is accepted silvicultural practice to leave unsaleable tops and branch-wood to rot. I now leave a fair bit of dead wood to rot where it lies under the trees in our garden spinney, and have instead coppiced one section to secure a supply of useful hornbeam poles in years to come. Regeneration of a tree for this purpose requires that it be felled, thus providing an immediate source of fuel. This spinney, however, in common with all the trees in the shelter belt which descends the hill from Lockleys Wood, has been under a Tree Preservation Order since 1954, so permission had first to be obtained from the County Planning Officer.

The work had the attraction of an historical precedent, for at one time all the woodlands hereabouts would have been coppiced. Some of our most cherished climax woodland, such as the New Forest and Burnham Beeches, reveals in the growth pattern of the mature trees the fact that perhaps a century earlier they had been coppiced or pollarded to yield a crop of poles.

Before the Forestry Commission began replanting in 1961, all seven of the woods on Lockleys Farm had been primarily native woodland, either naturally seed-regenerated or artificially maintained by the forester. Hornbeam predominated, with oak, ash, holly, wych-elm and cherry in irregular association, and birch as a fringe colonist. These species would have formed the climax forest growth if man had never come this way.

Here is real wealth, which like the rich man's money, grows while we sleep; but unlike that particular form of interest which is usury, the plant's growth does not derive from other men's labour. It accumulates at no cost to ourselves or our kind, and with benefits which can be enjoyed by all. The energy that falls on the roof of your house in the form of sunlight greatly exceeds the energy you consume in the form of expensive gas, oil, coal or electricity to heat it, but it is still unusual for any attempt to be made to trap this free source of energy – simply because the technology has been neglected. We have relied on cheap (but exhaustible) fossil fuel stocks in the earth, which have made the collection of solar energy look expensive in comparison. Fortunately for us, plants make no use of the economic expedient.

Whereas we find it difficult to convert the sun's radiation into a form of energy which can conveniently be stored, plants manage the trick very competently by photosynthesis, even though only 1 per cent of the energy received by the average temperate plant is 'fixed'. Even at this low rate of efficiency, plant annual production over the whole world is about 200 million tonnes of carbon converted from carbon dioxide into sugar, using no more than 0.2 per cent of the solar energy received by earth. The calorific value of all the energy mankind consumed in 1970 could have been matched by harvesting and burning just 5 per cent of the world's annual plant growth. In fact wood, peat and other vegetable matter supplied a significant 15 per cent of man's energy requirements in that year, and the proportion could rise if we restrained some of our more wasteful processes.

In country areas, return to a wood-fuelled domestic economy would bring another benefit in its wake: a revival of prolific woodland flower growth. Just as the cowslip and the fragrant orchid are receding on the farm meadow under pressure from hawthorn and dog rose, so a score of woodland flowers slumber in the woodland shade, waiting to be revived once the axe lets the light in. Cropping the woods on a rotation would enrich rather than impoverish them.

But the woodland on Lockleys Farm no longer produces an economic crop except where the Forestry Commission have planted their larch and pine. Coppicing for a pole crop has been abandoned.

When these woods were more highly valued, some hornbeam would have been allowed to grow to maturity and then be felled at an age between eighty and 150 years. The majority, however, were coppiced, that is, cut off somewhere between ground level and two or three feet high during the winter while the tree was dormant. In the spring, new shoots would emerge from the stools and these would then grow over a period of years into sturdy poles which furnished the crop. The process is akin to pollarding, in which the tree is cut off above the height at which cattle or other animals can browse the young shoots. The oaks were left uncoppiced to provide a shade canopy.

When Sir Edward Salisbury was traversing this countryside from his Radlett home in the early years of this century, preparing the data for his study of the oak–hornbeam woods of Hertfordshire, he could still detect the pattern of rotation which permitted thirty-four species of herbs to flourish under stools that had been coppiced two years previously (while twelve years' growth reduced the ground flora to a mere dozen species). Today the canopy has closed in and the uncut hornbeam poles have swollen to tree size, the origin of many revealed by the gnarled stool from which they have sprung, multi-trunked like a hedgerow reverting to forest.

In 1795 a writer noted the well-wooded character of Hertfordshire and recorded that these woods 'are cut in succession every ten years'. An 1804 edition of the *General View of the Agriculture of Hertford* refers to felling every twelve years when in the landlord's hands, but adds that tenants cut them every nine or ten years, so as to obtain the advantage of two crops in the twenty-one years' lease. By the time Sir Edward Salisbury arrived, he could still see that the shrub layer was coppiced at more or less regular intervals, but that 'many of the woods are often allowed to grow for a period of 14 to 16 or sometimes even 20 years'.

Hornbeam was once used extensively for sea defence works and for charcoal production, together with the more mundane sale for firewood, pea sticks and bean poles. The name means 'horny tree' and it is the hardest of the European timbers, as carpenters learn to their cost if they haven't got a saw file handy. It has been used in the past whenever a really hard wood was required, for such items as knights' lances, mill-wheel teeth, butchers' chopping blocks, buttons, mallets, ox yokes; it was the wood used by the early engineers to fashion cogs, pulleys and wood screws. It is still used for chessmen, for the tough inner rims of tennis rackets, for engineering wedges and for those parts of a piano which receive most wear; for skittles and skittle balls, golf-club heads and shoe lasts. The great drawback of the timber is that without chemical treatment it has very slight resistance to rot, and left in the open will crumble to dust within a few years. It has now largely been replaced by a wood from the West Indies, lignum vitae.

Revival of the hornbeam crop as a source of firewood, if nothing more, is certainly feasible through a return to rotational coppicing or pollarding of our neglected Hertfordshire woodland. The flora would be enriched even if the woodlands were less majestic than we now expect them to be. But rotation cropping needs organization and agreement, which hardly equates with *ad hoc* hacking of the poles. So what other sources of fuel exist? For me it was enough to use waste wood, which I found plentiful, both in the countryside and on the scrapheaps of local factories. But another source exists: the hedgerows. The importers of my Jøtul stove claim that 'if we learn to manage our hedgerows with the same degree of efficiency that we farm our farms, then the average farmer can be self-sufficient in firewood within seven years. By using our mechanical hedgecutters on the sides of our hedges, and by allowing the top growth to mature, we will not only have a surfeit of firewood, we will also obtain more shelter for outwintered stock, and earlier crops of grass and corn'.

At a time when hedges have been disappearing at the rate of 5000 miles a year in this country over the past twenty-five years, this may sound a belated suggestion, but there is now so much pressure on the farmer to relent, to cease grubbing out old hedges, and indeed to reinstate them in his own interest and in the interest of wildlife conservation, that the idea may well be valid.

To take a crop of poles from the top of a hedge means that during the intervening growth period it may effectively double its lopped height. Whether this is beneficial to the farmer depends largely on the nature of his soil. If it is dry and sandy, and he is growing a large-leaved plant like sugar-beet, then he will be better off with the tall hedge. Shading of the crop will reduce yield close to the hedge, but reduced transpiration from the crop and reduced evaporation from the soil through the check to wind speed will increase the yield over a distance equal to fifteen times the height of the hedge.

Under extreme climatic conditions, hedges need to be tall to give sufficient protection. To shelter the daffodil on the Isles of Scilly against salty Atlantic gales the fields are kept very small and the hedges rise up to twenty feet high.

I began this chapter by describing heat as the last gift of the tree, but the first and enduring gifts of wood are those associated with construction. Valuable as they remain in these days of sawn timber, it is only by entering one of those great tithe barns which have stood for centuries, that you can fully grasp the strength of wood that has been grown to meet the needs of the carpenter, which has been shaped with the wedge and adze along the line of the grain. Today we grow our wood in tight ranks to encourage tall, straight growth for planks, but the oaks of the New Forest, planted after the Napoleonic Wars, were heavily thinned to encourage a spreading crown. The need then was for natural crooks and 'knee' timbers to be used in shipbuilding, and there are good construction lessons we can learn from the shipwrights.

Shipbuilding made great demands on the structural properties of timber, and required large quantities of it too – as many as 5000 oaks went into the building of a man-of-war – but it was industry's need for charcoal that posed an even greater threat to the country's supply of wood. Acts of Parliament passed by Queen Elizabeth I in 1581 and 1585 sought to conserve London's firewood supplies against the demand for charcoal from the iron smelters of the Thames Valley, Sussex, Surrey and Kent. Elsewhere, prudent harvesting of coppice poles by the charcoal burners conserved the forests which were the source of their income and gave us an example to follow.

The commonly encountered domestic articles fashioned in wood by today's craftsmen include walking-sticks, clogs, hurdles and chestnut paling, trugs, osier baskets, butter moulds and, of course, furniture. But for the man who is not a craftsman the range is usually restricted to domestic fitments fashioned from store-bought planks. This irks me. I want to be involved in the fashioning of an artefact at an earlier stage, using the tree as a primary resource and not confining my work to the secondary product, the planed deal plank. I have a two-handed saw which I bought at a jumble sale for fifteen pence and then cleaned and filed back to a pleasing readiness for work. I have bought an adze and a draw-knife and have begun to learn a new craft. I do not pretend that I can fill every domestic need by my own efforts: even the smallest community develops some degree of division of labour so that those who have special skills can practise them. But I understand the yearning Thoreau felt, to spend part of a lifetime living frugally, making for himself the stool and the table to furnish the hearth that he had also constructed. 'For if I buy one necessary of life,' he wrote, 'I cheat myself to some extent, I deprive myself of the pleasure, the inexpressible joy, which is the unfailing reward of satisfying any want of nature simply and truly.'

It was natural that the use of wood as fuel should dominate my thinking initially, for warmth was a continuing need, whereas I already had more than enough store-bought artefacts to find it necessary to fashion spoons, bowls or a rolling pin from wood. So I consumed wood: green, seasoned and rotten; hornbeam, some ash, and later, wych-elm. To my delight I found that all were good burners – the hornbean and ash particularly. There is something of an art in tending an all-wood fire. Neglected, it can die down beyond revival in a very short time, although you left it blazing merrily. It is frugality that is the fire's undoing. As Herbert Edlin says: 'Logs like company. One will seldom burn well alone, but with two together the fire will rarely fail.' The ashes should also be left in the grate and not raked through to aid the draught. Then the whole bed of the fire holds the heat and feeds the flames.

If you have access to every kind of firewood (shunning only willow, poplar and alder) you may become a connoisseur of their smoke's aroma, even to the extent of devising log 'recipes'. But as soon as I had the little Jøtul stove installed and working efficiently, I resented the wasted heat going up the chimney of the open fire each night and reserved my logs for those evenings when we would most appreciate them.

The next practical use for my wood was in making bean sticks: a better end for brushwood than a bonfire. Then I constructed a shelter for the logs to keep the rain off while they were seasoning out of doors. If I ever had the need of a shelter for myself I hoped to have developed my skills sufficiently to keep the elements at bay.

The variety of uses to which wood can be put intrigues me,

and when I have exhausted all those of direct value I can still turn to others with an historic or curiosity appeal. There are comprehensive records of all the uses that every kind of wood has traditionally been put to. I like to think that some knowledge still has practical applications. When I whittled the teelers to hold my rabbit snares in position, I carefully chose unpeeled hazel rods as Richard Jefferies advised, 'no larger than the shaft of an arrow, and almost as straight . . .' Any other wood might have served the purpose, but hazel was the traditional wand preferred by the poacher, so that was the one for me.

The tree does not yield wood only. There are fruits, and nuts – and sap too. Birch-sap wine is a traditional drink in many northern countries, and one I want to brew. When the sap is rising in March, go out on a cold day and drill a $\frac{1}{4}$-in-diameter hole about $1\frac{1}{2}$ in into the bole about 12 in from the ground. Insert a tube (it could be a piece of elder with the pith removed) into the hole and put a receptacle underneath to catch the sap. No more than a gallon of sap should be taken from one tree, a quantity which may take two or three weeks to extract. Collect the sap every day, boil it and bottle it until you have enough for your brew, when you should remove the tube and plug the hole with wax.

The sap has lemon and orange peelings boiled in it for twenty minutes before sugar is added, and the yeast culture goes in when the liquid has cooled. Sycamore- and walnut-sap wines may be made in the same way. Birch sap is sufficiently rich in sugar to be boiled down to a candy, known as 'maple' sugar.

A more direct absorption of the tree's nutrients is possible by consuming the phloem, part of the cell layer encircling the trunk immediately beneath the bark. During the period of active growth in the spring, these cells are rich in proteins and carbohydrates, and I hope one day I will come across a recently felled specimen of a suitable tree, to strip a section and return to the kitchen to try it out.

Invalids with gastric disorders may still be given 'slippery elm' as a nutritious and easily digested portion of their diet. There is one particular species of elm (*Ulmus rubra*) from which this food is removed, but in North America the Indians used the phloem of a number of other trees as a source of food.

No doubt our ancestors found some European trees to be similarly nutritious. The phloem of elm, poplar, aspen, ash, lime and even pine could yield sustenance. I have chewed pine phloem raw, but the taste of turpentine made me spit it out. 'Bark bread' was made in Scandinavia until comparatively recent times, principally from elm (*Ulmus glabra*).

Wood has by no means gone out of our lives. Like so many other resources, it has simply been processed, using capital-intensive machinery instead of labour-intensive craftsmanship, and the end products, aside from lumber, are no longer recognizable as having stemmed from the tree: anti-freeze, synthetic rubber and food flavouring, DDT, sex hormones, Vitamin D and so on.

Egon Glesinger has suggested that wood consumption can provide a measure of living standards in the same way that a calorie count supplies a yardstick by which standards of nourishment may be compared between cultures consuming entirely different kinds of food. Just as a daily intake of 3000 calories is the optimum dietary standard, so a consumption of 3.5 tonnes of wood annually could provide an individual in an industrialized society with his entire domestic resources. No less than 70 per cent of this he allocates to meet the heat and energy requirements of a civilized standard of living. 'On the assumption that conversion to kilowatt hours and British thermal units is conducted efficiently and that the total energy yield is used efficiently,' says Mr Glesinger in *The Coming Age of Wood*, 'six tons of wood would cover the household's heating, cooking and lighting requirements.'

For those interested in calculating how much woodland is needed to supply their energy for the home, an acre of mature coppice woodland will yield a maximum of eight tonnes of green timber, the amount depending on the species and the number of years allowed between cuts (anything from ten to twenty years). A ten-acre woodlot managed with a ten-year rotation so that every year one acre is felled, should provide at least two tonnes of wood annually.

These are some of the possible uses of wood which you either own or forage. They challenge the amenity group attitude that a tree is a cherished pinnacle of botanical progress, a sacred symbol of inviolate nature. Trees are a crop. We should plant them for generations ahead, and we should harvest those that generations before have planted for us provided we do it in a disciplined way. The woods are a great resource, economic and aesthetic. Whatever route I take on my walks, they always lead me to the woods. I love them, but I use them, too.

## 10 The Roman snail

I may never know whether I am in truth a natural, born hunter, but as a gatherer I encountered meat in other forms. It was late in my first spring of phantom farming, returning from a cold, wet walk among the dying bluebells, that I first saw Roman snails in large numbers. Where the field had been ploughed tight up to the banked hedge of Lockleys Wood, a chalk escarpment provided the conditions they needed to thrive, just about as far north as they are found in Europe. On the path bordering the field of young wheat and on the leafy bank I counted fifteen snails in all, in a stretch of maybe 100 yards. They fascinated me. I soon realized that it was usually on wet evenings that I would come across them, always on this stretch of path (I later found a shell a quarter of a mile away, but have never seen a live Roman snail anywhere else on the farm.) Here indeed was a novel source of food . . .

I first tasted *escargots* in a restaurant in the West End of London, gristly pieces of meat in a highly flavoured sauce. Then I bought half a dozen in a *charcuterie* in Boulogne to be warmed in the oven until the garlic butter melted around them in their shells. After that I tried a tin of two dozen from a delicatessen counter. I wanted to have an idea of the commercial food against which I could set my own culinary experiences, and found them very tasty. The snails were certainly a resource of the clandestine farm, and one I was determined to savour. But they meant much more to me. To eat the snails became a symbol of liberalized taste in food.

I had been first amused, then fascinated by a little book titled *Why Not Eat Insects?* in which V. M. Holt exposed the prejudices which determine what we eat and what we reject. One culture devours a creature as a delicacy, while in another it is universally rejected with loathing. We eat scavenging animals like eels and lobsters, and reject fastidious vegetarians like cockchafers, caterpillars and wireworms. There's no reason for it, or if there is, it is one of culture and not common sense. So the argument went. In Africa, David Livingstone developed a liking for locusts and said he preferred them to shrimps. He would probably never have contemplated eating them if the opportunity had arisen in his native Scotland.

I had spent two years putting wasted resources to good use on the farm. The most useful were likely to be those vermin which preyed on the farmer's crops, like the corn-fattened pigeons we shot. But why stop there? If I so sincerely felt that the world could feed its people if they were only sensible and took what was available to them, then I should be prepared to make radical changes in my own habits.

Writing about synthesized foods such as separated leaf protein, Norman Pirie has stressed that supplying the foods to starving populations would be only part of the cure for malnutrition. It would be equally important to develop new cultural habits, or some people would starve while the new food lay, untouched, on their plates. Before it was introduced, a way had to be found to make a new food acceptable. It was necessary to explore how best to cook and serve it. And it was equally necessary for the introduced food to be surrounded by an aura of acceptance.

Dr Pirie did not confine his sentiments solely to the realm of spun soya, algae and oil-fed yeasts. 'Insects and other invertebrates are nutritious and might as well be eaten when they are available even though it may not be worth while expending effort on their deliberate cultivation,' he says. Like Mr Holt, he is conscious that 'irrational food prejudice is extraordinarily widespread'.

> In Britain, a chicken would be rejected long before it has putrefied to the extent considered proper with pheasant, raw oysters are eaten but snails are not eaten even when cooked and the pig is accepted but not the horse.

In fact, of course, snails *are* eaten. Only they are called *escargots*, they are usually imported, they are ridiculously expensive, and occupy a tiny niche in the present-day class culture, just as oysters do. It is interesting to consider that right up until Victorian times oysters were a staple food of the English working class, one of the few seafoods which poorer people in London could afford.

Professor Mary Douglas of University College, London, has suggested that food is used as a means of communication, as a signalling system and that is perhaps why we are so loath to change our eating patterns. It seems as though whoever provides the food is trying to tell us something when they innovate too drastically, and the message might be construed as a rude one. Another motivational researcher, Dr Ernest Dichter, says: 'Human beings have an appetite for the foods that symbolize the type of person they want to be. They have an aversion for foods that symbolize a type of person they do not want to be.' It is sad but probably true, that most people would consider any form of phantom farming as a regression, a significant start on the long slide back to the jungle, as unthinkable as picking up leftover vegetables in the gutter of a street market.

The investigation carried out by Professor Douglas showed that the traditional British meal is rigidly structured, permitting only minor variations in the constituents of the main meals, but she says: 'In the less structured parts there would be scope for introducing completely new kinds of food, new tastes and smells, cheap substitutes.'

A snack is defined as an 'unstructured food event', with no rules prescribing which items should appear together, which helps to explain why my own family will enjoy cockles and mussels from a stall on a seaside outing, but never fancy them at home where we rarely eat between meals.

Persuading them to eat snails wasn't going to be easy. But first I had to make the snails grow fat and multiply. Knowing that they are confined when bred for food, I constructed a rough enclosure roofed with wire netting, and brought a few of them back as breeding stock.

Country children used to sing:

Snail, snail
Put out your horns
I'll give you bread
And barleycorns

but mine fared better on the discarded outer leaves of cabbages, and lettuce (I planted young lettuce in the soil of the snail garden to provide fresh food when I was away from home).

In August I had five snails, and planted thyme and other herbs in the enclosure to introduce an element of automarination! In September I spread some chalk on one side of the enclosure to see if they would move to that side where the environment more closely resembled the one they had left. They showed little interest in either the herbs or the chalk-whitened sector of the cage. Returning from a week in Wales I found they had all disappeared. I suspected that they had departed through a hole in the enclosure I had overlooked, but thought it just possible that they had hibernated underground. I was chastened by the suspicion that I might have cut them off from the only ecological niche where they could survive. It depressed me that I had known nothing of them. They were aliens in my garden, prisoners in my private game. I felt I had deserved to lose them and only hoped they could regain an environment which would support them.

If we are to change our food habits, it must be an educational process. I began to educate myself. I learned that Roman snails are hermaphrodite, hibernate partly-buried for half the year, and need 20 per cent chalk content in the soil if they are to thrive. They retire into their shells to conserve body fluid, and are normally only active under damp conditions. They lay up to forty large eggs in an excavated underground chamber.

The following spring I built a new enclosure, a veritable *escargotière*, to house them in. They are not a communal species, their matings are haphazard and they have no contact with their young once the eggs have been laid. Nor do they appear even to have territorial instincts. I took just a few of the many snails I saw, to be sure that I was not depleting the stocks – which eventually I hoped to augment. When I had seven I took no more. None escaped this time.

One June afternoon I called on neighbours three gardens away, to collect laurel clippings which I hoped would grow for me into a hedge. Their seven-year-old daughter had been to see my snails earlier, and she called me to point out one she had found. Sure enough it was a Roman snail. I was so pleased, thinking it must be one of my previous year's escapees which had successfully survived the winter in its new territory.

We left the snail on the flower bed and went to look at her pet tortoise. We talked about burrowing animals, and I described how the Roman snail excavates a burrow for its eggs. She returned to where she had seen her snail and began to examine the ground minutely. Again she called me, this time to say she had seen an egg. Somewhat dubiously I went to look for myself, and there it was, close to the surface, a glistening white sphere almost a quarter of an inch in diameter, quite a bit larger than I had expected it to be. It didn't seem possible the hole it was in could contain perhaps two score of such large eggs; I wondered if perhaps the eggs were laid individually rather than in one clutch.

The next day was a Sunday, 30 June. Paul had shot a pigeon before breakfast which I wanted to pluck. I had a whole morning's work on the clandestine farm ahead of me, replacing the deadly nightshade (planted in error) with Good King Henry seedlings. There was much to be done. But the meadow was ablaze with yellow rock rose, there were wild strawberries to savour, and when it came on to drizzle a little, I found three Roman snails moving between the wheat stalks well away from the bank where their food plants grow. They are not known to make nests on cultivated land so I wondered if it might be the chalk lumps themselves they sought out, and whether they consumed the calcium neat to give them the mineral to transmute into new shell growth?

In the afternoon the sun broke through and I took my camera out to the meadow to photograph the fragrant orchids which were in full flower. When I had taken some colour pictures I walked on to the chalk outcrop to see if the snails were still around. As it was dry now I scarcely expected to see them, but a little way along the path I found three – one half-buried in the soil and two on the surface. As I crouched down to take a photograph I noticed a depression nearby just about the size of an adult snail's shell. I looked at it more closely. Down in its depth I could see three or four tiny snails, and on the edge, one on the move. It was not much more than a quarter of an inch across, a little larger than the egg. As I looked around more closely I saw there were a number of other tiny shells on the ground, some empty, some with the snails withdrawn inside.

There were no damaged shells. Perhaps it was temperature changes which had killed some, or starvation; down here on the corn-growing earth there could be few food plants for them.

Back in the *escargotière*, my captive snails had not been idle. I found one lying in a shallow depression, and lifting it off without encountering any resistance, I could see a nest full of white globular eggs – there could easily have been twenty or more. The snail had created a transparent veil of slime over most of the aperture. I took a photograph and replaced the snail. A few hours later when I looked again it had moved on, and the nest was covered over with earth. An incredible achievement for a creature with just one foot!

Later that evening another captive snail completed its nest of eggs, but after covering the site with earth one egg remained adhering to its body. I took it off carefully and put it in a test-tube with earth above and below, then sunk the tube in soil to provide an equable temperature. During the course of the next two weeks I examined the egg regularly, but although it was buried at an angle, rain got in and the egg disintegrated. Would the same thing happen to the eggs in the nest if it became waterlogged? It was occurring to me that under protected conditions the birthrate of the species might be impressive.

The Roman snail, *Helix pomatia*, is known also as the Apple Snail, the Vine Snail and the Edible Snail, but in fact it is no more nor less edible than other native British species. The Romans may have introduced it from the Continent, but there is said to be fossil evidence that it was breeding here already. Its culinary advantage lies simply in its size, and the Common Snail (*Helix aspersa*), which is closely related, is also eaten both in Britain and on the Continent. At one time snails were sold in the Bristol markets as 'wall-fish'.

By and large, snails have a reputation for being rather poor fare, and were often regarded as suitable only for consumption during Lent. But certainly for poor people who could afford nothing better, they were used as food all the year round – caught wild and fattened in snail gardens. Eleven per cent of their weight is protein.

At Chard, in Somerset, I talked to Mr Austin Wookey at Hornsbury Mills about his boyhood days working for a miller.

He used to be sent out to collect snails, and loved to watch the miller eat them.

'He would pop them in a pan of fat and leave them, wheezing and sighing until they were done, then winkle them out with the needle he used for sewing up sacks, dip them in salt and swallow them.'

The miller told young Wookey that snails were good for his breathing, and indeed they have had this reputation for centuries. Amongst many explanations given for their introduction to this country, a favourite stems from Sir Kenelm Digby's claim to have first imported them as specific medicine for his wife, who was ill with consumption. Millers used to suffer a lot from the dust they breathed, and despite the pints of cider they drank to wash the dust down their throats, Mr Wookey recalls that in his experience they developed a complex network of veins on their faces and usually died young.

In the West Country the snails were taken from the crevices of walls on the hills while they were hibernating. 'You didn't eat them at other times because they were full of vegetable matter. You waited until they had sealed off their entrance,' says Mr Wookey. The Miners' Arms restaurant at Priddy in the Mendips has built its reputation on the snails it serves, cooked in cider and herbs.

M. S. Lovell's advice on preparing snails, collected a century earlier, is still the principal source of culinary information and is widely quoted even by an authority such as Elizabeth David in her *French Provincial Cooking*. Lovell provides some fifteen detailed recipes and many accounts of associated sauces. Nor does he neglect the needs of the gatherer as distinct from those who buy their snails in the market.

> When first the snails are gathered from the hedges, etc., it is a necessary precaution to starve them for a few days, and not to eat them at once, as they feed on poisonous plants, such as the deadly nightshade, poppy, datura (*thorn-apple*), etc.; cases of poisoning by snails having occurred where they had been gathered near, or had fed upon these noxious plants.

Madame Millet-Robinet, the Mrs Beeton of mid-nineteenth-century France, advised leaving snails to starve for at least one month in a cool, but not damp place.

I followed the Italian custom of keeping the snails in bran, which they are supposed to eat, but made the mistake of leaving the bran-filled box in the open, with just a loose-fitting lid to deflect rainfall. The bran went mouldy and some of the snails died. Those I had left in the snail garden buried themselves with just a white epiphragm showing where they had sealed off the mouth of their shell.

They are effectively storing themselves, while in this hibernating state, which lasts from the autumn until late April or early May. The French consider the season for snails really begins after the wintering mollusc has been nipped by the first frost in October or November.

Like other shellfish, snails are cooked by dropping them alive into boiling water. When Dr Ernest Pollard of the Nature Conservancy exhibited some of the Roman snails he was studying, I heard a little girl visitor say to her mother, 'I wonder what they taste like?' and receive the perfectly matter-of-fact answer, 'whelks'. But not all mothers could be that objective. Most would probably imagine a scene such as that described in an old book called *Curiosities of Food*, in which a Dr Black and a Dr Hutton were confronted by a dish of stewed snails.

> Dr Black *at length* 'showed the white feather': but in a very delicate manner, as if to sound the opinion of his mess-mate. 'Doctor,' he said, in his precise and quiet manner, 'Doctor, do you not think that they taste a little – a very little – green?' 'Green! Green indeed! Take them awa'! Take them awa'!' vociferated Dr Hutton, starting from the table and giving full vent to his feelings of abhorrence.

If snails should be available in quantity – and a walk in the country on a rainy summer's evening reveals how common they are – I see no reason why they should not be used as the meat constituent of stews, casseroles and pies, using wine and herbs to marinate them and supply liquor for the recipe; or simply as fuel food, minced as an ingredient in sausages, risottos, rissoles, curries and so on. Like this they could be introduced surreptitiously! Not surprisingly, in view of the price of commercially supplied snails, existing recipes present them as a gourmet item, with nothing to disguise their origins. Taking advice from a variety of recipes, the consensus is that the snails should be put in boiling water (preferably with charcoal) and kept simmering for fifteen minutes. You should then remove them from their shells and wash them thoroughly. There is a little bit of hard matter (the jaw) which should be cut out of the head, and the small intestine – which emerges from the mantle above the snail's body – is removed. In addition to the traditional French presentation with garlic butter, you could try these recipes:

*Stuffed with herbs:* replace the snails in their shells with a mixture of salt, pepper, salad oil, rosemary, thyme, parsley and winter savory, all shredded small, and bake over a gentle fire.

*Fried:* flour the snails and fry them. Serve with a sauce made from butter, vinegar, fried onions, parsley, orange juice and slices of lemon.

The end is not yet. After snails, which I find quite palatable, I'll try caterpillars. And why not?

I look for butterflies
That sleep among the wheat:
I make them into mutton pies,
And sell them in the street.

For me, the Knight's song in *Alice Through the Looking Glass* is almost a prediction come true.

# 11 Winter

As another winter drew in, the plants on the meadow died back, leaving rowetty tussocks of dead grass standing clear of the ground, and just the green patches of salad burnet which would stay fresh and tasty to chew even when frost lay thick on the leaves. I ate some as I left the meadow behind and walked up the edge of Lockleys Wood.

It was a mild November morning. This side of the footpath field had been newly ploughed, the job abandoned, half done. From close up, the furrow slice presented a smooth, shining face where the ploughshare had carved the soil. The uniform brown of its distant appearance was now clearly seen to be mottled in places by the brighter browns of a clay stratum or the white of chalk. I was amazed how these mineral disparities in the soil had survived a century of ploughing.

All nature seemed to be enjoying the last of the mild days before winter. As I walked across the pigeon-gleaned fields of barley stubble where chickweed was fast encroaching, flocks of chaffinches flew up and made for Foxley Grove. The tree profile in shades of copper and gold was alive with animated silhouettes of all kinds of birds: blackbirds, thrushes, a magpie, and suddenly a flock of some eighty wood-pigeon taking to the wing.

On through the thickets of Hazel Grove. Not a regular route for me; I had been here searching for – and failing to find – the hazels and I had picked shaggy parasol toadstools, but otherwise the leafy canopy was too dense, the clearings too restricted for the wood to offer many resources for me. Farther on still lay Puttockhill Wood. I entered by slithering under a wire fence to reach the one track which traverses it. There was very little timber at this point, it was all spindly coppice and thorn, intractable scrub. On the map the path is shown as running as straight as a fire-break, but in fact it meanders so much that I soon lost any sense of the direction in which I was heading. At one point I was confronted by a barrier, the shoots of a briar having been skilfully woven across the narrow path, necessitating an eye-threatening detour through low and twiggy scrub to regain the ride. In the end, Puttockhill Wood defeated me. I emerged right back where I had entered it, at a point diametrically opposed to the exit I sought. I tried again, this time diving straight through the low, bushy hardwoods which formed a shelter belt at the perimeter, planted closely enough to form a good first line of defence. I breasted a rise covered with tall, wet brake and, looking upwards, spied a pair of goldcrests high in the branches of a larch copse.

Deep inside the wood was a fairytale land carpeted with hornbeam leaves, and these in turn overlaid with the bright, fallen needles of the larch.

We need a guide through these woods, someone with the confidence to reassure us when the path seems to lead us from where we think we want to go. And yet how often when we hearken to the guide do we find that our confidence in him was misplaced. Am I in need of guidance, or am I finding out – here under the larches – that I am the guide, learning how to lead? Who is the guide, which is the goal?

I was not looking for anything on this day. I was conscious of the season, and of where I was, and I was alert, like Ortega's good huntsman.

All that day I had been detached from reality; I felt myself to be an observer – not disinterested, for I was intensely aware of everything that happened, but not involved. I had lifted the rotting sacks which covered the compost heap in my garden and discovered two woodmice, which appeared to ignore this rude intrusion and carried on a whisker-twitching assessment of their environment for several moments before scampering away. And later, sitting on the ground on the first rise of Puttockhill Wood, I watched a milk float crawling up The Avenue on Mardley Hill across the valley where the old Great North Road set off for Stevenage. The little blue and white vehicle looked from this distance like some bright beetle making its tortuous way over a log which had fallen in its path. As it reached the steepest section of the road the few milk crates it carried began to slide towards the tail of the vehicle. Still the milkman drove on, and the crates fell silently to the ground. Then the float stopped and the milkman climbed out and surveyed the smashed glass and white rivulets which ran down the road, as the sound of splintering glass came crepitating to my ears, distant but amplified by the dished hills. Powerless to act, far enough away to be removed from the faintest possibility of involvement, yet I was aware of every detail and nuance of the event.

So I view the folly of my fellow men when they live their lives divorced from the woods and fields. Sometimes I am quite estranged from their action, as when helplessly I watch politicians or businessmen take a further step away from the path I tread, and the signing of contracts is shown on the television screen or comes as a newspaper report which leaves me feeling limp. But sometimes the action is that of a neighbour or a friend, and despite our proximity I sense my attitude as being so distant from their own that I might aptly clap a reversed telescope to my eye and project them to a distance where their actions and their arguments could fall hopelessly out of synchronization like the sound of the breaking bottles, so little difference would it make to the sense. When we disagree, I sometimes think to myself, it is because we are talking a different language, or talking about two very different subjects. I can agree with everything you say if I can only think with your mind. You can accept everything I suggest providing I avoid the introduction of any idea the equivalent of which is not already stowed in your signal locker.

At half past three the sky was blue, overlaid with a tracery of clouds that seemed unrelated to it, not just at different levels but on a different plane, so complete is the segregation. Over there, cumulus. Cirrus streaking in high from the west. And scudding in fast from the north, skeins of grey raincloud. Plateaux, towers, arrisses of cloud, a magnificent orchestration of vapour that presages rain. No English watercolour this, where each hue would be laid on white to give a transparent glow, but a kaleidoscope of overlaid colours, each scene achieving a darker sky as it runs in like theatre flats and backdrops.

In the woods is perpetual youth . . . Within these plantations of God, a decorum and sanctity reign, a perennial festival is dressed, and the guest sees not how he should tire of them in a thousand years. In the woods, we return to reason and faith. There I feel that nothing can befall me in life – no disgrace, no calamity (leaving me my eyes) which nature cannot repair. I am the lover of uncontained and immortal beauty. In the wilderness, I find something more dear and connate than in streets or villages . . . The greatest delight which the fields and woods minister, is the suggestion of an occult relation between man and the vegetable.

When Emerson wrote that, America was a land governed by men who craved a population to bring about national growth. All they had to give the settlers was land, and they gave it cheaply. Now the wilderness has shrunk and while man hunts down the last of the pests which deny him the full use of land – the mosquito, the tsetse fly, the locust – he is helpless to deal with the next pest, which is himself.

What is so sad is the reinforcing effect of folly. When society is built on a false premise, such as the concept that land can be pre-empted by those with the money to purchase or the power to protect it, then any rational suggestion must be dismissed as nonsense before it threatens the foundations of the edifice. When everyone is mad, the sane man is dangerous and must be locked in an asylum.

Under a system which permits a man to have and hold more land than he alone can plough and harvest, and thus unjustly denies millions access to the soil which would nourish them, the only tolerable reaction is to infringe those hollow property rights, to take what the law calls 'adverse possession' of it whenever this can be done by stealth, and to trespass as and when the spirit moves us.

To visualize a better life when there are no immediate precedents at hand to emulate, calls for a special kind of imagination. Without it, all roads to utopia seem impassable. There is apparently a law which provides that those individuals most readily available to build utopias, prove the least well-equipped to do so. Nevertheless, the worth of their work is in no way diminished by their almost inevitable failure. To the ranks of vagabonds, gypsies, mouchers and other travellers we can add urban and country squatters, land reformers and other inheritors of the philosophy of the True Levellers or Diggers: '... So long as we, or any other do own the Earth to be the peculiar interest of Lords and Land Lords, and not common to others as well as to them, we own the Curse, and hold the creation under Bondage.'

Gerrard Winstanley, a leader of the Diggers, had a vision in a trance, telling him to publish it abroad that 'the earth should be made a common treasury of livelihood to whole mankind, without respect of persons' but the Diggers were routed before ever they could establish their free communities.

In a modern assessment of their philosophy, Christopher Hill, former Master of Balliol College, Oxford, says that 'Winstanley's conclusion, that communal cultivation of the commons was the crucial question, the starting point from which the common people all over England could build up an equal community, was absolutely right.'

Collective cultivation of the waste by the poor could have had the advantages of large-scale cultivation, planned development, use of fertilizers, etc. It could have fed the expanding English population without disrupting the traditional way of life to anything like the extent that in fact happened. The Diggers sowed their land with carrots, parsnips and beans – crops of the sort which were to transform English agriculture in the seventeenth century by making it possible to keep cattle alive throughout the winter in order to fertilize the land. 'Manuring' is the crucial word in Winstanley's programme. ('True religion and undefiled is to let everyone quietly have earth to manure.') Winstanley had got a solution to his own paradox: 'the bondage the poor complain of, that they are kept poor by their brethren in a land where there is so much plenty for everyone, if covetousness and pride did not rule as king in one brother over another'.

That opportunity has gone, never to return, for the rout of the Diggers heralded the age of enclosure, and the commons and wastes were acquired at first in part, and eventually almost in total, by the large landowners. The law parcelled the land most meticulously among those with claims, but the cost of enclosure and increasing poverty meant that the small husbandmen had to sell out. Once the lands were concentrated in a few hands, the established custom of primogeniture served to keep estates intact, the eldest son inheriting. It was all done legally, but many saw it as simple appropriation from the have-nots by the haves, summarized in an anonymous verse:

The fault is great in man or woman
Who steals a goose from off a common;
But what can plead that man's excuse
Who steals a common from a goose?

I began this book in the open air, describing a personal initiative inspired by those early free enterprisers of the countryside, the sturdy vagabonds. I end it in the company of philosophers, in the sphere of politics and economics. Many will dismiss all that falls between these extremes, and the extremes themselves, as inflammatory nonsense, or dangerous subversion. I know the arguments well. I have rehearsed them, sometimes respected them, even been cowed by them. They do nothing to make me alter my views. Land is not to be owned outright. This demand can never be suppressed, no matter what confusion or calamity might ensue were it to be met.

I can accept that I may not live to see the day of reform, but for me there can be no easy way back: the other life will always be the one which feels strange, and feeling as I do I cannot be silent or withhold encouragement from any of the same persuasion.

My winter's walk took me down to Turpin's Ride then on to Footpath 30 through Harmer Green Woods, but I left it soon to trace a well-grassed path, skirting a plantation of Corsican pine. Deeper and deeper into the woods I walked, the path wandering and narrowing. I took out a small compass from my pocket to see whether I was maintaining any one direction, but the pointer was dislodged. I carried on, bending lower to make progress through the unbrashed branches, my scalp needled by the trees. Finally I emerged near the railway and sought a way back through open fields where the cycle of ploughing, harrowing and planting was complete.

To the west, a rich, port-wine sunset, which faded abruptly as the full moon came through clouds behind me. I was in the familiar bowl of ploughed fields, sure of my route, but failing to comprehend the relationship one to another of the fringe of black woods all around me. Gone were the little land rises which daylight would have revealed, or the differentiating shades of wheat and barley which gave each field a personality in summer. It was all anonymous and strange.

There was still some blue sky left, and in the broadest part of that blue a single star shone. I walked on and on, amazed by the alien landscape, the featureless prairie of ploughed earth. Then I noticed a scrap of paper on the ground and stooped to pick it up. I could make out some words on it: 'Mergamma . . . Mercury . . . do not handle unnecessarily . . . wash hands . . .'

I was back on Lockleys Farm.

And now they cry out the Diggers are routed, and they rang bells for joy: but stay, Gentlemen, your selves are routed, and you have lost your Crown, and the poor Diggers have won the Crown of Glory.

# 12 Roots

Standing on Lockleys Warren I strive for a sense of being, of oneness with the land and all that lives on and from it. My ears distinguish perspectives of sound. At first the persistent working calls of a family of bluetits – newly hatched and hunting in the trees – dominate everything else, but soon I can draw in from the distant fields the pigeons' murmur and the lilting skylark song. Somewhere halfway between these, the squawked protest of a jay suddenly fills the middle distance of the auditorium. It is a scenario to place me where I belong, on the earth but not *of* it, as an earthworm is of it; moving on one plane only, breathing an atmosphere that the birds sport in, in the air but not *of* it as they are. Everything I hear is above me, where I aspire to be, but cannot reach. But what of the sounds of the earth and the creatures that live in it? I scarcely hear anything quieter than a grasshopper. Did you know you can hear a snail eating a cabbage leaf if you listen closely? What noise does a worm cause as it drags a leaf segment into the ground? The earth soils me when I touch it, its smell is neutral. What I cannot see or hear is likely to be beyond my comprehension.

When David Thoreau decided to live alone in the woods above Walden Pond and practise self-sufficiency, he stayed for two years. 'I went to the woods because I wished to live deliberately,' he wrote, 'to front only the essential facts of life, and see if I could not learn what it had to teach, and not, when I came to die, discover that I had not lived . . . I left the woods for as good a reason as I went there. Perhaps it seemed to me that I had several more lives to live, and could not spare any more time for that one.'

Thoreau did not trespass – he had no need to – but the reason he had for living at Walden Pond had been a motive for me, and in starting my experiment I expected to abandon it in time for the same reason which caused him to return.

But I cannot leave, unless my new life permits the same land access. However many other lives call me, I will return to the land. Not only for love of this piece of earth – another could supplant it in my affections – but from a conviction that there are riches here we must not abandon. These wild plant resources differ subtly in quality and composition from their hybridized descendants; how can we be sure that shop-bought provisions supply every element and chemical combination our bodies need? Doctors deal in sickness, but health is our own concern, and we enjoy good health through the agency of plants.

What I saw when I walked over the farm was superficial, just like a modern flora that illustrates only the aerial growth of plants. The illustrators who provided woodcuts and engravings for the early herbals may have stylized their plants into conventional patterns with some loss of accuracy, but at least they showed the plants whole, complete with roots. The bright yellow roots of nettle, the dangerously fragile white worm-like roots of bindweed, the deep plunging column of a dock's tap root, are as individually characteristic of each plant as its leaves, even if we must pull it to know it. It is by these roots, as much as by the photosynthetic activity of the leaves, that we survive.

The more I study plants the more I hold them in awe. They may lack the ability to see, smell, hear, taste, feel or move but what they achieve without sensory perception or movement makes my life possible. I am what I eat, and to presume that physically I am in any way separate from my environment, simply because I walk on the earth instead of growing in it, is clearly untrue.

There is little I can do for the plant kingdom which supports me, and those human sensory attributes I have listed have become a means to aesthetic appreciation of life rather than tools for survival. If I seek self-reliance in the wilderness all my senses support me in one way only: they lead me to identify resources which will supply food, shelter, clothing and fuel – and the source of almost all of these is the plant kingdom. So much vegetation do I consume directly, or indirectly through the food chain of the animals that are slaughtered for me to eat, that I need to be able to move to find new supplies. My animal strength is that I can be a parasite on plants.

Technology has not freed us of this role. Despite years of study, scientists are still unable to reproduce the chemistry of photosynthesis in the laboratory and we still rely on the mineralized deposits of plant life long ago transmuted into coal and oil for our fuel. The heat of the sun warms us by day, but the tree can use that energy to grow. When the sun goes down we throw another log on the fire.

An animal is a compact entity. It is normally of a shape to make efficient, swift movement possible. A plant is quite different in concept. It has no need to be compact because it is not going to move. Instead it is diffuse. The area of all the leaves on a tree is vastly greater than the ground area shaded by its crown, but the root system may be even more impressive. The roots of a single plant of winter rye were found to measure 387 miles when they were finally unravelled from the two cubic feet of soil in which they were growing. When root hairs also were included in the calculations the length reached nearly 7000 miles, with a total surface area of 7000 square feet.

It is the surface which the plant presents to its environment – whether it is the leaves in the atmosphere, or the roots in the soil – which is important, for though the plant may represent a concentrated resource to the man who eats it or burns it or builds with it, it has become so only through accumulating diffused resources: carbon dioxide in low concentrations in the air, sunlight which may arrive through a cloud layer or be reflected from other surfaces, and the dilute mineral nutrients in the soil.

In simplified dietary terms we speak of vegetables supplying us with carbohydrates and vitamins, while the fat we need comes from dairy products and nuts, and meat gives us protein. This presentation of our needs obscures the fact that carbohydrate (in its simplest form of glucose, $C_6H_{12}O_6$) is present in some degree in all plants, but for the most part, it is a 'building block' for the more complex molecules, the fats, proteins and higher carbohydrates which contribute to each plant's individuality. Of the ninety or more chemical elements found naturally on earth, twenty-four have functional roles in living organisms and we ingest most of these through the agency of plant roots.

Plants which can photosynthesize carbon dioxide into carbohydrate also prove to be efficient miners. Our efforts are crude and inefficient in contrast, for it requires high concentrations of minerals before our methods become worth while. Emmanuel Epstein points out that iron is that metallic element mined by man in the greatest quantity, and it is not economical to extract it unless the iron content of the ore is about 30 per cent. 'Potassium is the metallic element that plants extract in the greatest quantity. More often than not it is present in the soil as a concentration of less than 1 per cent.'

And yet the plant is able to concentrate significant quantities of minerals during its growth period. One of my favourite wild vegetables of the chalk meadow, salad burnet, contains 2 per cent magnesium, although this is an unusually high concentration.

Analyses of wild plants show great variation in their constituent parts. Sir Edward Salisbury records that rosebay willowherb may contain twenty-four parts per million of cobalt, that dandelion may have fifteen ppm of copper, and both dandelion and stinging nettle 300 ppm of iron.

'These data emphasize,' he says, 'the insurance that a diversity of species of herbage may provide against deficiency in any one respect.'

The quantitative value of the plant kingdom in terms of resources is phenomenal, but it is the quality, the usefulness of the resource that is immediately available to us that concerns me more, and was the motive for my aberrant research.

Nothing that sustains the plants is denied the animal kingdom. We breathe the same gases which they inhale, but far from nourishing us, we exhale as waste the very stuff of their life: carbon dioxide. We dig the soil, rub the crumbs between our fingers, and the mineral wealth trickles away from us. We have to plant before we can reap much of that wealth.

The simples which herbalists have commended through the centuries to their ailing contemporaries drew on a wide range of plants, and therefore a wide range of mineral traces. The basis of each plant's reputation was partly alchemy, partly an application of the doctrine of signatures – whereby, for example, iris petals would be used as a poultice on bruises because their colour resembled that of the bruise – and partly the distillation of centuries of experience. This last factor ensured that the plant comfrey earned a reputation as a bone knitter, which was later scoffed at until the active healing ingredient allantoin was identified in it. But it is my guess that regular and diverse ingestion of benign wild plants of itself ensured that the herbalist and those he treated preserved the basis of good health.

Diets were apparently monotonous right up until the sixteenth century, when the practice grew of fetching medicinal herbs from other regions. 'I have seen in some one garden to the number of three or four hundred of them, of the half of whose name within forty years past we had no manner of knowledge,' wrote William Harrison in his *Description of England* in 1587. Still, those who could afford to eat well, ate meat, and the seventeen volumes of Evelyn's *Acetaria: a Discourse of Salletts* only arrived in 1699 to extol the virtues of the freshly plucked leaf, and to make the herb a food for the healthy as well as a medicine for the sick.

In my browsings over the vegetable kingdom I have paid no particular attention to the so-called herbs, which I class as the plants with a noticeable content of volatile oils or marked flavour. The herbalists made use of a wide range of wild plants, and so made a wide range of trace elements accessible. Commercial man opted for the fat crop and began the process of selection and protection that goes by the name of agriculture today. Only in a few instances now, such as watercress, does the cultivated plant bear a close resemblance to its wild forebear, though even the genetically evolved hybrids derive from wild stock originally. Nor is it simply a question of improvement by selection. To quote G. W. Dimbleby in *Plants and Archaeology*: 'True cultivation nearly always results in detectable genetic differences as compared with the wild parent.'

It is said that no major crop has been brought into cultivation from the wild during the past 5000 years. Cultivation of the forerunners of today's crops by prehistoric man made it possible to feed ten times the world population that subsistence living could support, and for this reason if no other, subsistence living can only be for a few who are lucky enough to have access to sufficient land. But an emphasis on the greengrocer as the only link we have with the produce of the land is mistaken, wasteful and, I suspect, may prevent us from developing our full potential of well-being.

Can anyone say that we know every requirement of the body? I believe that if our diet is extensive and includes natural foods (untreated commercial crops, plus 'wildings') we won't need to know what our diet should include. Nature will provide.

In this spirit I ranged the farm, conscious of the need for agriculture but critical of expedients that reversed the old farming philosophies. What they used to say was: 'Live as if you are going to die tomorrow – farm as if you are going to live for ever.' Now they stand that adage on its head.

The virtues of the farmer's crop are so often selected to benefit the farmer, not the consumer – or the land. A species is planted because it has a 'flush' and can be harvested economically, or because it has a thick skin and will travel without sustaining damage, or because of its size. Rarely do factors like flavour or nutrition or soil-benefit outweigh the rest.

I shall grow the vegetables that give me the flavour and sustenance I want, and when I run short will certainly buy from the greengrocer; for all *I* know, his plants may be as good as mine! But when it suits me, I will walk the farm and pick nettle and salad burnet, Jack-by-the-hedge, and wild strawberry, to cast my net wider in the genetic pool. What do I stand to lose, and how much might I gain?

Plants which were once important to the countryman have not all disappeared. Fat hen, the rampant weed of the new road verge, was once of sufficient domestic importance for villages to be named after it. The plant was formerly known as melde, and the place name of Melbourn near Cambridge is simply a corruption of the plant name. No one today would find it difficult to bring it back to the table.

The field archaeologist (called a dirt archaeologist by his library colleagues who prefer to delve in manuscripts) keeps a keen eye open for plant 'indicators' which may suggest the site of former habitations. Surveying the lost village of Box near Stevenage the forester/historian W. O. Wittering searched for sainfoin 'grown in the past for fodder and, as a result of past cultivation, it still flourishes there'. Wittering was looking for evidence of a churchyard and quotes with evident satisfaction the observation of a writer in 1728 that 'St. Foyne grows very kindly in that consecrated ground.' He continues in his report:

> Another interesting 'indicator' is a colony of the rare Green Hellebore (*Helleborus viridis*) in the south western corner of the wood. Such colonies may exist as relics of cultivation from abandoned gardens. It was grown by housewives as a cure for boils, spots and worms.

These links with the past give an historical perspective to the 'wildings' I garner. Each and every one is descended through generations just as people are. Archaeology and buildings provide a tangible link with our past, but plants, like people, offer a genetic link. Whereas contact with the fabric of buildings and the memories of people permit us to *feel* towards the past, plants permit us to feed on it. The food which sustained my ancestors is still here – unaltered, if it is a wild food – to sustain me. The thought excites me, I feel impelled to consume these historic ties!

Now I stray to the limits of folk lore. There are few records of how peasants used potherbs, and when you delve further back the gulf between cultures past and present conceals culinary shocks. In his book *Archaeology by Experiment*, J. Coles writes:

> There have been relatively few attempts to experiment with the food of prehistoric man. It may be that erstwhile experimenters are too cautious to subject themselves to the possible damage or indignities caused by the consumption of exotic, ill-prepared or downright inedible foodstuffs.

There is no need to look far for an explanation of that reluctance. We can see culinary gulfs between living cultures without having to look to the past. We have already speculated that the family who once might have regarded oysters or snails as the protein portion of their staple diet will now find such fare disgusting, an eccentric and expensive foible of a decadent aristocracy dining out. At the seaside I always treat my sons to cockles or winkles; a foot-in-the-door to keep taste sensations catholic against the relentless commercial pressure to close them to almost everything but the fishfinger, the beefburger and the frozen pea.

No one will eat wisely if they are not prepared to eat widely. Even the lowly cabbage can cause goitre if eaten to excess, and to over-indulge a taste for onions may cause anaemia. Bananas contain serotonin, and a diet depending too much on that one fruit would be a diet laced with poison. Variety is the key to good nutrition.

I cannot say whether wild food is important in maintaining good health. Who can prove this when well-being stems from a whole spectrum of environmental and hereditary factors overlaid by fortune? What I eat may be good for me. But more important, it keeps me alive to the knowledge of what I *can* eat. No strikes or disasters leave me worrying where my next meal will come from. It will come from the earth, whether other men bring it to me, or I go out alone to find it.

In a hungry world this knowledge – that food exists, away from the market and the fruit stall – can literally be a life saver. The world is short of conventional food, but life-sustaining alternatives derived from wild plants can counter starvation providing the ignorance and prejudices of mankind are overcome. People do starve in the midst of plenty both through lack of knowledge of what they can eat and through a reflex of revulsion that prevents them stomaching it. One man's delicacy elicits disgust in another. Until we all cultivate an objective appreciation of what is edible we should not criticize those races who reject new food on grounds of religious or cultural dogma.

It is not the place of the underprivileged always to be innovators when the food runs out. It is rather more likely that the privileged will be more rational, better educated, more adventurous in considering the elements of their diet. This point is made by Norman Pirie in paving the way for a dietary revolution in the Third World. The facts must be known about new foods and the fallacies must be disproved by those best able to refute them. Who is ready for this task?

People never have had freedom of choice in nutrition. With the best of intentions their parents misled them in their youth and, with more questionable motives, advertisers mislead them in adult life.

In the countryside there is no special pleading, no partiality, no compulsion. Here are natural resources and much is known of their value. We can admire them as curiosities or use them as once they were regularly used. I used them for many reasons, not least of which was a desire to avoid the trap of convention. But I also had a desire to extend myself, to use all my senses, develop every skill, to live as a man, and to teach my sons that man is of the world, not a creature apart. While the earth provides, I taught them, we will be provided for.

In today's economy such talk is subversive, for it shatters the myth of the money system. I make no apology. Paul Goodman once wrote: 'It is desperately hard these days for an average child to grow up to be a man, for our present organized system of society does not want men. They are not safe. They do not suit.'

I will never accept that it is the role of society to shape me. On the contrary, I am free to shape society if others are of a like mind to help.

You will make your own judgment upon my success or failure as a clandestine farmer. I am content with my enterprise. There exists a grass clearing in a wood where Good King Henry is sparsely naturalized and some comfrey plants have their roots well down. Such bracken as remains could fairly be called vestigial, and I root it out when I visit because what I have I want to hold; I could not oppose the territorial impulse in others so strongly if I failed to recognize it in myself.

Here is where I made my connection with the earth, and even though I never took a crop from the holding, its fitness to be planted increases with every season. The grass is forming roots, and the roots will improve the soil structure and increase its fertility. This land is ready for the plough.

I am told that imaginative planting could have included pignuts, wild carrot, wild garlic and wild radish, but this would have made my plot a herbal oddity rather than a food resource. I'll find my herbs by foraging. Meanwhile my vegetables grow on plots which were once almost as neglected as that clearing in Foxley Grove, but I have no need to approach them with stealth. My new territory is made up of scattered plots of urban wasteland, long-abandoned allotments, part of a churchyard, widows' gardens. To make them productive and share the produce with the tenants is most satisfying.

When we have learned to use our urban wasteland, then is the time to look again at the countryside and ask ourselves, is it right for some to have land while others are landless; should there not be a parity of earth as of air and sunlight? When the consensus is for common rights, they will follow, and the words of Winstanley will be read as prophetic truths.

# Bibliography


## Chapter 1

OVER THE FENCE

White, Gilbert, *The Natural History of Selborne*, (1789), The World's Classics, Oxford University Press 1902, page 197. The matter alluded to is the use of rushes instead of candles.

## Chapter 2

LOCKLEYS FARM

Blake, William, *Auguries of Innocence*, about 1803.

Mabey, Richard, *Food for Free*, Collins 1972.

Emerson, R. W., *Nature, the Conduct of Life, and other essays*, Everyman's Library, Dent 1963, page 67.

Szczelkun, S., *Survival Scrapbook 2*, Unicorn Books 1972.

Forsyth, A. A., *British Poisonous Plants*, HMSO 1968, page 3.

North, P., *Poisonous Plants*, Blandford Press 1967. Published in co-operation with the Pharmaceutical Society of Great Britain.

Dimbleby, G. W., *Plants and Archaeology*, John Baker, page 26.

Masefield, G. B., Wallis, M., Harrison, S. G., and Nicholson, B. E., *The Oxford Book of Food Plants*, Oxford University Press 1969, page 190.

## Chapter 3

FORGIVE US OUR TRESPASSES

Bailey, R., *The Squatters*, Penguin Books 1973, page 37.

*Working Party on Vagrancy and Street Offences, Working Paper*, HMSO 1974, pages 13–14.

*Daily Telegraph*, 3 January and 6 January 1975.

*The Observer*, 9 March 1975.

*Royal Commission on Common Land 1955–8*, HMSO 1958, page 98.
Hoskins, W. G. and Stamp, L. Dudley, *The Common Lands of England and Wales*, Collins 1963.
Simpson, A. W. B., *An Introduction to the History of the Land Law*, Oxford University Press 1961, page 3.
Hoskins, W. G., *The Midland Peasant*, 1957, pages 193–4.
Jefferies, R., *The Gamekeeper at Home* (1878), The World's Classics, Oxford University Press 1948, page 48.

## Chapter 4

PRIVATE LAND AND COMMON RIGHTS

Johnson, W. B., *Industrial Archaeology of Hertfordshire*, David & Charles 1970, page 86.
Hudson, W. H., *A Shepherd's Life*, Everyman's Library, Dent, page 282.
Pasmore, A., *New Forest Commoners*, published by the author, 1969, page 13.
Campbell, I., *Law of Commons*, Commons, Open Spaces and Footpaths Preservation Society 1973, page 25.
Hoskins, W. G. and Stamp, L. Dudley, *The Common Lands of England and Wales*, Collins 1963.

## Chapter 6

HUNTER'S MOON

Murton, R. K., *The Wood Pigeon*, Collins 1965, page 150.
Lishman, M., *A Pigeon for the Pot*, The Wildfowlers' Association of Great Britain and Ireland 1971, page 11. One of a collection of thirty-four recipes from the Midlands Woodpigeon Club.
Gasset, José Ortega Y, *Meditations on Hunting*, New York: Charles Scribner's Sons 1972.
Shepard, P., *The Tender Carnivore and the Sacred Game*, New York: Charles Scribner's Sons, pages 122–3.

## Chapter 7

AUTUMN

Ramsbottom, John, *Mushrooms and Toadstools*, Collins 1953.

## Chapter 9

THE WOODS

Williams, H. A., *Poverty, Chastity and Obedience: the true virtues*, Mitchell Beazley 1975, page 71.

Stubbs, A. E., *Wildlife Conservation and Dead Wood*, a supplement to the Quarterly Journal of the Devon Trust for Nature Conservation 1972, page 5.

Salisbury, E. J. (1915, 1918), 'The Oak-Hornbeam Woods of Hertfordshire', *Journal of Ecology*, 4, 83–117; 6, 14–52.

Thoreau, H. D., *The Journal of Henry Thoreau*, (1906), Dover Publications 1962. Entry for 22 October 1853, page 639.

Edlin, H. L., *Trees, Woods and Man*, Collins 1956, page 110.

Glesinger, E., *The Coming Age of Wood*, Secker & Warburg 1950, page 72.

## Chapter 10

THE ROMAN SNAIL

Holt, V. M., *Why Not Eat Insects?* (1885), E. W. Classey 1969, pages 30–31.

Dichter, E., *Handbook of Consumer Motivations*, McGraw-Hill 1964.

Douglas, M. and Nicod, M., *New Society*, 19 December 1974, page 744.

Lowell, M. S., *The Edible Mollusca of Great Britain and Ireland, with recipes for cooking them*, L. Reeve & Co. 1884, page 226.

## Chapter 11

WINTER

Hill, Christopher, *The World Turned Upside Down*, Temple Smith 1972, pages 104–5.

## Chapter 12

ROOTS

Brinkworth, B. J., *Solar Energy for Man*, The Compton Press 1972, page 220.

Epstein, E., *Scientific American*, May 1973.

Salisbury, Sir E. J., *Weeds and Aliens*, Collins 1961, page 366.

Wittering, W. O., 'Deserted Medieval Villages in Hertfordshire', *Hertfordshire Past and Present*, 4, 1964, Hertfordshire Local History Council, page 14.

Coles, J., *Archaeology by Experiment*, Hutchinson 1973, pages 48–9.

Pirie, N. W., *Food Resources Conventional and Novel*, Penguin Books 1969, pages 166, 175. Copyright © 1969 by N. W. Pirie.

Goodman, P., *Growing Up Absurd*, Random House 1956, page 14.